Civic Youth Work
PRIMER

D1712285

This book is part of the Peter Lang Education list.
Every volume is peer reviewed and meets
the highest quality standards for content and production.

PETER LANG
New York • Washington, D.C./Baltimore • Bern
Frankfurt • Berlin • Brussels • Vienna • Oxford

Ross VeLure Roholt and
Michael Baizerman

Civic Youth Work
PRIMER

PETER LANG
New York • Washington, D.C./Baltimore • Bern
Frankfurt • Berlin • Brussels • Vienna • Oxford

Library of Congress Cataloging-in-Publication Data
VeLure Roholt, Ross.
Civic youth work primer / Ross VeLure Roholt, Michael Baizerman.
pages cm
Includes bibliographical references and index.
1. Youth—Political activity—United States.
2. Political participation—United States.
I. Baizerman, Michael. II. Title.
HQ799.2.P6V453   306.208350973—dc23   2013005246
ISBN 978-1-4331-1881-4 (paperback)
ISBN 978-1-4539-1113-6 (e-book)

Bibliographic information published by **Die Deutsche Nationalbibliothek**.
Die Deutsche Nationalbibliothek lists this publication in the "Deutsche
Nationalbibliografie"; detailed bibliographic data is available
on the Internet at http://dnb.d-nb.de/.

The paper in this book meets the guidelines for permanence and durability
of the Committee on Production Guidelines for Book Longevity
of the Council of Library Resources.

© 2013 Peter Lang Publishing, Inc., New York
29 Broadway, 18th floor, New York, NY 10006
www.peterlang.com

All rights reserved.
Reprint or reproduction, even partially, in all forms such as microfilm,
xerography, microfiche, microcard, and offset strictly prohibited.

Printed in the United States of America

Table of Contents

Acknowledgments vii

Chapter 1
Mapping Civic Youth Work: The Field 1

Chapter 2
Contesting Youthhood: Living Youth Citizen(ship) 19

Chapter 3
Civic Youth Work: The Program 51

Chapter 4
Doing Civic Youth Work: The Practice 73

Chapter 5
Civic Youth Work: The Practice of Civic Youth Work(er) 93

Chapter 6
Evaluating Civic Youth Work 109

Bibliography 123

Index 141

Acknowledgments

We believe that all publications are collaborative efforts. This is very true for this primer. We are grateful to those who have shared with us their stories, wisdom, and, when available, evaluation and research data about the work they have done or are doing with young people to support democratic, community, and social development. This work often goes unnoticed and rarely gets named as a vibrant and worthwhile endeavor. We begin by thanking our colleagues and friends from around the globe who continue to invite and support young people's participation on personally meaningful and consequential public issues in Jordan, Northern Ireland, The Netherlands, Qatar, Syria, Canada, Finland, United States, Laos, South Korea, Morocco, Jordan, Palestine, Egypt, Israel, Uganda, Croatia, Turkey, Ireland, United Kingdom, and South Africa.

We are also hopeful. The practice we describe in this text comes from real-world examples, which are having real-world impacts. The ongoing and vibrant invitations and support that young people receive in many locations give us hope that tomorrow will be better for them and for all of us.

Finally, we thank those that have given us support and solace as we have worked on this project, our partners, Christine VeLure Roholt and Jeanne Forbes. We could not have finished this project without you!

1

Mapping Civic Youth Work:
The Field

Sartre prodded people to assume responsibility for themselves and their world, demanding that they see their own links with systems that injure others—demanding that they recognize themselves as active subjects, and urging them to participate consciously in their societies and their histories. (Aronson, 2012, p. 17)

Caveat lector! Let the reader beware! We have organized this primer more for scholars and students than for practitioners. We faced a choice: Present the theoretical grounding of this practice and then derive from this civic youth work practice, or present the practice and then use theory to make sense of the practice. We have chosen the former, following convention and the larger purpose and style of this primer series.

However, we tweaked the convention in two ways: First, we begin with a description of an ongoing civic youth work project, letting the practice show itself and inviting the worker, coauthor Ross VeLure Roholt, to tell a bit about what he is/was doing and why. Second, we add to that narrative a short introduction to evaluating civic youth work so as to keep practice and evaluation close. A challenge to this can be made from the position that any case example is only an example of a larger class of phenomena, and that any evaluation should and/or could be a way of getting at the case, the larger class, and the theory undergirding the work.

Our response is given in Chapter Six, which discusses more fully the issues and foci of evaluating civic youth work.

Civic youth work as we conceive it is not an "it"—there is no "there" there! Rather there is an ethos and craft orientation towards young people as citizens. There are adopted (often adapted) knowledge, practice, and skills from many sources—wherever we and others find good ethicomoral civic practice, with young people and others.

Over time we expect that if "civic youth work" as a name continues, and if workers come to be named by others and by themselves as "civic youth workers," then there may come to be a material civic youth work, along with the rhetorical, symbolic, and metaphorical civic youth work now existing. We are against the reification of civic youth work, this way of seeing youth and doing youth work. Thus caveat lector!

This book is our address to you; we look forward to your response.

Civic Youth Work: Practice Narrative

It takes too much space to describe the work I have done over the last three months with young people on a youth arts program evaluation within a municipal parks and recreation system. Instead, I provide three vignettes to introduce my practice at three times: the beginning, middle, and end. Of course, much of this linear description is misleading, since groups and civic youth work continually recycle—from idea, to planning, to action, to reflection, to replanning (an adaptation of action research and collaborative inquiry (Reason, 1993)). Good civic youth work recreates democratic space (VeLure Roholt, Baizerman, & Hildreth, 2013) for young people to continually be engaged and act upon public issues that are personally meaningful.

Vignette 1: Beginning

The room where we meet is located in an older municipal parks and recreation building. It was repurposed a couple of years ago by young people, and made into a youth art space which has supported youth art workshops, a youth art gallery, and open-mic nights monthly for spoken-word and other youth performance artists. Early on, adult staff supported a youth-leadership group to provide advice and guidance on the building's art programming. At the beginning of this project, I asked the leadership group's youth worker if the group might want to work with me on evaluating youth art programming across the parks and recreation system. The youth worker said I could come and invite their involvement, and the members would decide if they wanted to work on the project and with me.

I arrived at my first meeting with the group ten minutes before its scheduled start. Three group members were there talking about what had happened in school that day and what had happened last weekend. I was greeted by the youth worker and introduced. The youth worker started the meeting by asking the now five members (out of eleven who belonged to the group) what they wanted to add to the meeting's agenda. As ideas were added, more members began to arrive, each greeted by those already there. At different times, several members would get up and run over to give someone a hug and ask about their day. By the time the agenda was set, all eleven members were there.

Early on in the meeting, I was asked to introduce myself and my project idea. I talked about working at the university, and wanted to know if the group wanted to help me with a youth art programming evaluation project. Silence; eventually someone asked what they would be doing. Unfortunately, I described their role as helping to create an observation evaluation tool, conducting field observations of youth art programs, talking about what they saw, and writing up what we learned for others to read. Silence; then a group member commented, "sounds a lot like school." I smiled, knowing I had chosen the wrong way to describe the project, and the group was telling me politely that this is not really what they would want to spend their time doing. My time on the agenda was almost up, so I asked if they would think about it and if we could talk about it next week. Fortunately, they agreed.

The second time I came to the group differently prepared. I started by asking them to tell me about how they became interested in art. The group told truly amazing stories of how they were supported and encouraged to do art by family, friends, or others (some teachers, but mostly community art instructors). They talked about how hard it was to stay motivated, and said that if it were not for their art friends and programs like this, they would have a much more difficult time doing their art. After everyone told their story, I asked: "Does having the opportunity to learn about art matter? Does it matter to you, or is it simply another hobby that might turn into a career?" Again, the group talked about how art and good art opportunities supported their personal and social development and improved their overall physical and mental health. Art was not just "something that they did"; it allowed them to be "who they are." I then asked: "Would you want similar opportunities for other young people?" They answered, "Yes!"

I talked about how the proposed evaluation project was about being able to take a stand on what good youth art programming should look and be like. If they chose to participate, they could help to shape youth art programming for the entire municipal parks and recreation system. They talked some about how they would want this, since most of their art experience was at community parks and recreation centers, and, in their opinion, existing programs were not well done or of high quality. They wanted to help to make art programs throughout the city better and more accessible to other young people. Now they were excited, and eagerly agreed to help evaluate youth art programming at community parks and recreation centers.

Vignette 2: Middle

We had been talking about good art programming and education, how school-based art courses often diminished their enthusiasm for art, and what programmatic elements and practices are basic to any youth program—for example, an adult who listens to young people and cares. As we talked, it became clear that several group members had a clear understanding and experience of good art instruction, while others had wisdom and even expertise in working with elementary-aged young people (many had worked at summer camps, and one member had started a small business as a school-age day-care provider).

As we continued talking about their experiences, I continued to ask questions about how we could incorporate what we were learning in our talks into a way (tool or instrument) to observe youth art programming citywide. Quickly, they created questions to bring with them as a guide when observing—what they should look for and look at—and to help them gather observational data at each site. By the end of the meeting, the first observation tool was drafted. I then asked if they wanted to engage in practice observation sessions to determine whether or not the method we figured out worked. They agreed that such practice observations would be helpful. Over the next week a team of members went to one site to see what was going on, and they "gathered data."

Vignette 3: Ending

After they had gathered the data, I asked the five members who did observations to describe what it was like to go and watch, and what they saw at the site. They first talked about how weird and uncomfortable they felt initially, "observing" other young people doing different art work, and about the experience of being watched by the young people at the site (an R. D. Laing (1970) experience).

Then they talked about what they found troubling—a lack of coordination among teaching staff, inappropriate comments made by an art instructor, too much time focused on art activity without some time allotted for trips to the restroom or to get a drink of water. Others joined in and talked about related personal experiences and art opportunities that were similarly organized and facilitated; this helped to clarify what troubled the observers.

After several minutes, another group member, silent until now, responded to my question— "What else?"—by saying that she also saw a lot of things that were done well. Others agreed, and began to talk about and describe what they understood to be things the program had done well, and what they hoped other staff would replicate at different sites. They talked about how all young people were encouraged and could participate, the caring interactions they often saw between staff and young people, and the variety of art materials that were available and accessible for participants to use creatively. Once everyone seemed to have talked about the observations, I asked: "What did you learn? And what do we do with what we have learned?"

This narrative tells a brief story of civic youth work, emphasizing the interactions and cocreative process of starting a project with young people. The narrative also highlights the important questions in evaluating this practice. What should the evaluation focus on? How should an evaluation of this practice be designed? Can this work be evaluated if the civic youth worker has not yet mastered civic youth work? These questions raise important topics and issues when designing and implementing an evaluation on civic youth work. At issue is a simple idea—How do we know when the practice is ready to be evaluated (Chapter Six)? Simply observing the practice and/or measuring individual youth development outcomes may not provide enough data to make a judgment on the practice's worth or value (the purpose of evaluation). Also important is whether and how the practice created a democratic youth space, and supported a democratic way of living. What makes these elements difficult to evaluate is that they are often embedded in tacit and implicit knowledge.

Civic Youth Work: Tacit and Implicit Knowledge

While the narrative just described is organized on the surface in a linear fashion, the work was less so; narrative form shaped the presentation, a classical concern in field studies, including ethnography (Wolcott, 1999). Presented is one cycle of the work: from idea, to planning, to action, to reflection, and replanning. In this narrative, the cycle from creating an observation tool, to completed observations, to discussing these, led to redesigning the tool. This linear or cyclical read is just one way of presenting what happened. Alternatively, we could have presented a decision narrative, one not so worker-focused, or a consequence narrative, attending to the question of "so what?"

In this narrative, the practice emerges. For example, we hear how the civic youth worker (who also was there as an evaluator) initially missed his opportunity. He poorly described the possible project, instead of proposing it in a way that made sense to the young people and connected to their experience. His description made the project "sound a lot like school," like something they did not want to do. The worker, rather than seeing this as their final answer, asked to come back again. He then more thoughtfully planned his next presentation. Here, we witness how practitioners both reflect-in-practice and reflect-on-practice (Schon, 1983), adapting what they do and how they do it based on the group's response. He learned both (a) that what he did at the first meeting did not work—the task remained unclear and unconnected to the young people, and (b) how to more effectively talk to them. When given the opportunity, he found that the second approach worked, and group members agreed to cocreate and in other ways participate in an evaluation. This narrative shows that good practice can be described and understood narratively, and hence is available for critique and teaching.

That some claim that civic youth work is ineffable, that this practice cannot be described and understood, must be challenged. It is not epiphenomenal, nor does it exist in a nether world, inaccessible and resistant to the uninvited or uninitiated—to outsiders and strangers. This position is extreme, and is put here to mark one end of a continuum on which civic youth work practice can be described— the pole of "it can't be told simply and clearly" for several reasons: It is too much an art; it is "intuitive"; or its practitioners are simply not able to or trained to describe what they do, how and why, and to what effect(s).

A strong challenge to this position is the work directed at making explicit **tacit or implicit knowledge** (Göranzon, Hammaren, & Ennals, 2006). Tillberg (2006) argued that it is by using examples that a practice can be "developed and established" (p. 166). Through examples work can be named, and submerged layers of knowing and doing can be made explicit, then taught and learned. Indeed there is a long history and rich literature on tacit knowing (Polanyi, 1958) and implicit knowing (Underwood, 1996). To get at practice, to describe and analyze it, is basic to naming and developing a field, program, and a practice.

Civic Youth Work Field: Program and Practice

The field of civic youth work can be understood as constituted by civic youth work programs and civic youth work practice. This is how we organize this text, and we use these two constituents as frames for explaining the Big Picture (program, project, initiative), i.e., what civic youth work is as idea, ideology, structure, and content; and for describing and analyzing civic youth work practice—the civic youth worker and "the work"—the ordinary, mundane youth work which, with additions, is civic youth work.

The text moves back and forth between and among ideas, concepts, narratives, and analysis, showing that civic youth work, as we conceive of and practice it, is a dynamic (Aristotelian) **praxis** (Guy, 1991). Civic youth work is a moral practice ethically carried out, joining the moment to theories, concepts, and understanding(s) of youth/young people/young person; to our take on activism/engagement/participation; to our perspective and practice of social action/politics; and also to our understanding of citizen/**lived citizen(ship)**/citizenship/life and "public work"—citizen work (Boyte & Farr, 1997).

By the end of this book, the reader will have been given a short, deep, theoretical, and (somewhat) practical primer on our grasp of the civic youth work field—program and practice. A reader, at the end of the book, could say, "So what? There is little here that is new." We agree! What we do is bring together and highlight what is an old practice across time, place, type of government, form of democracy, and much else. Indeed, this is our contribution, we believe: To make what was present but unnoticed visible, clear, and consequential.

The Three-Legged Stool: Youth, Citizen, Youth Work

This primer sits on three legs: youth, citizen, and youth work. This is how we construct civic youth work, its practice, and its practitioners (civic youth workers). We locate the three first in three different domains and finally in a single field: civic youth work. We did this by first providing a direct civic youth work narrative about current work (above). Second, in Chapter Two, we provide theoretical and philosophical definitions of each. Third, we present a set of three programmatic descriptions of civic youth work initiatives, projects, and programs (Chapter Three). We read each narrative to explicate the three nodes of interest—youth, citizen, and civic youth work. These beginnings are then used to explicate civic youth work practice and civic youth worker (Chapters Four and Five).

This serves to introduce two forms of reporting a practice—its ordinary, mundane, everyday ways of working; and the more abstract, programmatic home within which direct, hands-on practice is done. Taken together, direct civic youth work practice and civic youth work program/initiative/project show the United States field of civic youth work. A goal of civic youth work is to move from its status as "program, initiative, or project" to "the ways things are typically done around here"—a shift that illuminates the sociopolitical and cultural change which makes ordinary this form of youth work.

Youth work and civic youth work

An observer of typical **youth work** and civic youth work, who could not hear what young people and a youth worker were saying, would have difficulty telling the two apart. If they could hear the worker and young people talk, they might be able to discern the difference between the two craft orientations. It would depend on whether or not the civic youth worker and group were talking civic youth work. What does this mean?

Practically it means that

1. Civic youth work is a close sibling or cousin to most forms (nonclinical) of youth work;
2. It is difficult to tell these forms apart simply by (looking at) their activities and processes; and
3. To be civic youth work it must be named in a language that makes more or less explicit that an end goal of the work is the young people's experience of and reflection on their work as a group and individually, and that it is public, civic, citizen-work: They have lived citizenship (VeLure Roholt, Hildreth, & Baizerman, 2009).

Is this true for us even if the worker and young people together and alone do the same activities, talk the same talk, and do the same work? YES! Why? Because to name all of this is to place it in a frame, a way of doing and being, making all of this identifiable, easy to see and hear, and to claim for oneself the role of "citizen." As an informal pedagogy, a learning strategy, the primary goal and/or outcome is for the young people to have tried out a citizen way of being and doing; that means to name the ways of being and doing. Once claimed, these ways can be told to self and others, and in these small ways, work to open more spaces for young people to be called to be citizens and to do citizenship—on issues which matter to them and to others, and to do citizenship for themselves and for others—friends, community, and more. To name is to bring into a different existence.

This conception, demand, and/or requirement fits for us with our understanding and belief that civic youth work has no essence, only essentials, one of which is to be named as such. This means to us that there is not a pure, distilled practice that works as a touchstone against which other practices can be tested for purity—

political or methodological correctness, or philosophical or ideological rightness. What is present and does not change is that it is a valuational and/or ideological practice grounded in the values and group practices of open, democratic, inclusive, just, respectful, and meaningful work together on issues, topics, concerns, and/or problems that meet this same test.

In other contexts—national, institutional, sociocultural—this conception will likely be challenged aesthetically and/or politically as not fitting "how things are done around here, now." We do not ask for universal acceptance of our view and practice; just that alternatives be put into conversation with our notions. In this way, we do not define civic youth work for all, but our conception can become a touchstone for clarity—not purity—about other ways of conceiving of and practicing civic youth work.

Most basic are the civic youth worker's ethos and craft orientation: To bring about and sustain the ongoing conditions, context, and/or environment in a small group so that the young members can be exposed to and begin mastery of citizen roles, applicable now to their citizen involvement and also over their life course. How is this done?

First, civic youth workers must be clear about their own ethos and craft orientation, and accept this as their primary work. They must not work with the young people as if they were "clients," students, adolescents; not as if they "need help," in the human service sense. Civic youth workers must take on a citizen-making **gaze**—seeing and bringing about a citizen training and rehearsal space. This is not an intentional therapeutic space, or a school classroom or performance space for the worker or their trainees. It is profoundly a citizen learning space.

Second, civic youth workers must have a vocabulary for their civic youth work, and it must be appropriate to the work. For example, we have observed young people doing quality civic work, but who could not tell us what they were doing, why they were doing it, how they thought about their work, and how they actually did the work. It may be that some hold that a citizen should not be held to this standard of articulateness as a citizen, even as a youth. We disagree. Citizen-ness, citizen-ship, and self-as-lived-citizen all require a civic language of participation and engagement, and we believe this to be crucial and necessary, in part to ensure that personal and social values come to be inextricable from the self as citizen, and to the selection of issues to work on (helping to define what is good, bad, needing repair, and awaiting birth).

Third is the issue of time in civic youth work. Democratic practice takes longer than nondemocratic practice, when done right and fully. Civic youth work is deliberative in its ethos and practice, with time made available for "talking it out."

Indeed, this is where language is brought back—youth simply need words to do this, a common vocabulary—preferably, we believe, a social action/citizen/political vocabulary. Time becomes problematic in highly regulated time-space systems such as schools, and this works to push civic youth work toward technique and away from long and deep talk; "time pressures" create different routes to citizen and different types of citizen. Ideally, civic youth work "should take as long as it does." Time in schools and other host organizations is also bound by the school and organization calendar: school is out, group is over.

These three themes in doing civic youth work suggest that the civic youth worker does not teach "about" being and doing citizen, but rather teaches first to be and do citizen. The civic youth worker accomplishes this by being, himself or herself, an example of this. There is talk, choice, decision, reflection/talk, action, talk/reflection/evaluation, adjustment, and revision. Civic youth work, as we conceive of it and practice it, is a grammar of citizenship.

What Is the Big Deal?

A book on civic youth work perforce must itself address the subject of youth civic engagement—the active involvement of young people on public issues of interest, concern, and meaning to them. This is not a Big Deal either in conception or practice. But it is treated as such. The apparent (and alleged) low rates of young people doing civic youth work in a variety of formal social institutions (e.g., political) and practices (e.g., voting) have led to concern about the "future of democracy" and future civic life and civic society, and, more powerfully, to moral panic (Thompson, 1998) about young people's "**civic apathy**," noninvolvement, nonparticipation, and nonengagement in and disengagement from everyday, local civic life.

How can we bring young people back to institutionalized, everyday, local civic life? One response was new and expanded civics curricula (Pratte, 1988). Then there are policies inviting, and structures supporting, "youth involvement" through advice giving (Percy-Smith, 2010), and through membership on adult-dominated boards of directors of adult-funded and adult-managed youth (serving) agencies and programs (Zeldin, Camino, & Calvert, 2003). Others focused on youth voter registration and education efforts (Simon & Merrill, 1998). Still others proposed increased service-learning and volunteerism (Battistoni, 2000). And finally, practical school- and community-based projects (and other structures) in which young people are invited to learn how to be involved as citizens doing "public work" (Boyte & Farr, 1997) on meaningful issues of importance to them. There are many proposed pathways to civic and political engagement.

Our work is grounded in this reticulum, whether it is seen as civic education (Niemi & Junn, 2005), citizenship education (Davis, Gregory, & Riley, 1999), experiential education pedagogy (VeLure Roholt, Hildreth, & Baizerman, 2008), action learning, youth action (Linds, Goulet, & Sammel, 2010), youth participatory research (Cammarota & Fine, 2008), social reform (Schutz & Sandy, 2011), political education (Hahn, 1998), youth activism (Ginwright, Noguera, & Cammarota, 2006; Kennelly, 2009), politics, or, as we prefer, youth civic engagement. A major distinction within this field are those authors and practitioners who focus on young people as future citizens (S. Bennett, 2000), and those who understand young people as citizens now (Checkoway, Richards-Schuster, et al., 2003)— our position. Some of these authors ignore, and others valorize, young people as "youth." All have sought to create curricula to support youth civic, citizen, and political education around the globe.

Many writers and practitioners give their attention to "curriculum" for teaching, learning, and the mastery of citizen- and/or public-worker skills and related attitudes, values, and knowledge. A few highlight the role of adults (or youth) doing the teaching and training (Kirshner, 2006). This is one of our primary foci: the person who, regardless of formal title—teacher, coach, youth leader, or community volunteer—can, when doing this work, be a Civic Youth Worker (doing civic youth work). Most curricula developed tend to take the worker for granted, and assume that the curriculum works when implemented correctly. The worker only needs to be technically competent in delivering the curriculum as designed, and youth civic engagement will be supported. Most often, we have found this not to be the case (Hildreth & VeLure Roholt, 2013).

We attend to the substantive issue about youth citizen involvement; the moral panic about youth noninvolvement, nonparticipation, or nonengagement; and to youth as idea, as age-graded population, as a developmental idea and "stage," and as young person(s). We focus on "programs" and/or curricula used to enhance mastery of and lifelong citizenship. We look closely at how these efforts work. Throughout, we look at the role and practice of civic youth work. We drill down in deeper explorations about how to evaluate civic youth work, an increasingly necessary and potentially useful practice. Included will be empirical studies that support the effectiveness of youth civic engagement. This, too, is now crucial when soliciting funds, and for practical evaluation.

We are interested in the mundane, everyday practices of youth civic engagement, such as those examples we give through and in this vignette: A friend's junior-high-aged daughter (12 years old) and her friends wrote and presented to their school principal a group petition about one of his decisions on a school dress code.

These girls took for granted their citizenship, with its right to organize and petition to address grievances—this was for them ordinary, everyday stuff, albeit exciting, fun, and consequential to them, their friends, other students, school faculty and parents, etc. There is no big deal here, only a disclosure of citizenship, and the social and cultural conditions which invite and support it (or not).

Why This Book?

Civic Youth Work (CYW) is a youth work **craft orientation** (Bensman & Lilienfeld, 1973), simply one approach to doing good work with young people. It is neither magical nor mystical. Rather, it is ordinary and mundane, everyday work with young people—but with a difference. There is nothing weird about it or its practice. It is simply good work with young people in small groups on issues which matter to them and about which they want to "do something." What gives CYW its kick, its symbolic jolt, its sort of outsider-ness, is that it is intentional practice that is intentionally read as "political," i.e., it is about power, intentional social change, groups of youth, conflict, and the like—all words with political resonances, with high-octane meanings in our (and other) societies: youth being political (citizens) and doing politics!

In our society, in contrast to many others worldwide, we are not accustomed to images of young people as child and adolescent soldiers, often with weapons taller and bigger than they. Our students are now unlike those at foreign universities who hold mass demonstrations, and close their schools. We do not often see images of young people needing medical care, food, water, clothing, and safety (and care, and love, and . . .) as a consequence of civil conflict and war. Communally, we have forgotten images of those youth who embodied the U.S. Civil Rights Movement, by sitting at the counter waiting to be served ice cream, being beaten by police, praying in church and on the street before a march in the name of equal access to schooling (Levinson, 2012). We do not have at hand and at the front of our collective memory many images of young people as "activists," as social reformers, as citizens.

We see and can remember young people in their exotic, subcultural, sartorial performances, their unusual hair styles and bricolage in dress; we do not recall the ordinary, mundane images of young people as a group helping elderly neighbors rake leaves or shovel snow from sidewalks and roofs. In general, we remember better the unusual, the exotic, the frightening, more than the typical, ordinary, and mundane. We forget the youth serving us at a fast-food place, or the one helping our grandparent at a nursing home. We remember the kids standing together—a gang?—at the corner, and especially so if they are different than us in race, ethnicity, social class, or style; especially if we perceive them and experience them as frightening.

Youth doing civic engagement—working together on issues of meaning and importance to them—do not elicit such memories or responses. Mostly, they are invisible, and if seen, these are the "good kids" doing "good work" and "good works." These kids are like Boy or Girl Scouts—different, we are taught to believe, in upbringing, parenting, work ethic, personal responsibility, and in other ways, moral, just, good, and right: these are our "better future," our "best kids," we are told.

Civic youth work is about the sociomoral requirement that every young person should be invited to contribute to the everyday life of his or her community. It is about the cocreation and cosustentation of open and inviting local structural opportunities for such engagement (Percy-Smith, 2010). Also it is about the moral compact among youth, community, and those who work with and on behalf of young people that young people be guided in their mastery of citizen expertise, especially in intentional and reflective small-group action. Civic youth work is about bringing all of this together in ways that invite and support young people as citizens now, as well as lifelong. All this is done not simply for the enhancement of individual, healthy, and/or positive development, but for a larger, more overriding purpose—the ongoing resuscitation of communal civic life, particularly democratic civil society—for its reproduction and its improvement. It is here where possibilities exist for the true reciprocities of youth and community (and communal) development (in terms meaningful to members of both).

This book is not about magic, or mystery, or the exotic. It is about the (almost) invisible—the collective practice of small-group work with youth that is grounded in young people's interest, concern, commitment, and desire "to make a difference" to something larger than self or friends, i.e., "to make the world a better place."

> The Black students we talked to in class were surprised by our presence, because the White people they encounter typically shun them or fear them. They were not at all accustomed to having White people ask them questions. And they did have opinions. Their views were most intense on issues related to diversity and to local law enforcement and the court system. These teens pay almost no attention to what is going on in the world, apart from issues that directly touch their lives or the lives of their family members. Civic engagement and political participation are completely alien notions to them, yet they were lively when asked to express their views, and eager to share their experiences with us. Very little is standing in the way of their good citizenship, other than the fact that no one has come along

to tell them that their voice matters, that someone is listening. We concluded that in order to become engaged, these youth simply had to be asked. No one around them, however, was doing any asking (Gimpel, Lay, & Schuknecht, 2003, p. 5).

Here is a source of our conception of civic youth worker, to be "the one around them," inviting them into civic engagement, into their citizenship. We change the words a bit, while the idea is the same: *Civic youth work is the (worker's) embodied invitation (on behalf of a community) to join-in to "make a difference" on "issues which matter to you."*

The models of civic youth work and youth civic engagement we discuss and promote are culture-bound in the deepest sense. These are rooted in the secular, individualistic, liberal West/North, with its traditions of (relatively) free, voluntary associations (de Tocqueville, 1966), free speech, group advocacy, parliamentary democracy, and the like. All of these are both source and bedrock for civic youth work practice—which is, *a priori*, value-based. This is in contrast to other social reform, social action, and sociopolitical cultures within nations, as seen in the first Arab Spring (2011) movements and the recent (2012) group attacks against the US by some Arab activists who claim that "freedom" in political and civic discourse means the right not to be belittled and labeled as a religionist, or to many, as a nationalist; this is even more so when religion and state overlap legally and/or culturally, as in perception and practice (Kirkpatrick, 2012).

In practice, this means that ours is a poor reference to other models, styles, and protocols of civic youth work and the civic youth worker, and that civic youth work and others who would take on this role must modify our ideas and suggested practices to meet local realities. All of this is obvious, but must be said (other examples are found in VeLure Roholt, Baizerman, & Hildreth, 2013).

Reading Youth Civic Engagement

The language game of civic youth work is civic engagement. The core concepts are: youth work, civic youth work, youth, youth civic engagement, citizen, citizenship, lived-citizen, civic society, civic life, civic action, and social capital. All are closely, if not inextricably related, conceptually if not always in everyday talk (depending on the society and the historical moment). One can read each term through the others as a way to get at their relationship, and to disclose and explicate those relationships between and among them not easily noticed.

Read "citizen" to get at "youth." When citizen refers to voting rights, then "youth" becomes a chronological age, typically 18 years old for eligibility in governmental elections. Seen here is the obvious but often overlooked: citizen is an age-graded concept and practice. Since citizen is so closely related to "civil society," and since citizen is age-graded, civil society, too, can be read as an age-sensitive concept and reality. This suggests attending to how youth are invited and supported in the civil society they live in, and asking how age works (or how age is used) to create or deny opportunities for youth involvement in civil society and in youth age-graded institutions, such as schools, sports, religious and spiritual spaces, at work, and of course, at home.

More abstractly, *citizen and civic life disclose the standing of young people in their society*. For example, if citizen is a basic role in society, and young people are denied this role opportunity solely or largely because of their chronological age, then age as such is a criterion for sociopolitical and socioeconomic citizenship, as with voting. If this is so, can a strong critique of current civic life policies and practices be made on the ground of age? Or is age simply a proxy for income or something else? Could it be that time as such and age as such are proxies for a person's "readiness" or an individual's "capacity" for engaging in civic life? Are all of these proxies for what is now called "development," in its "ages and stages" formulation?

This Stuff Is Real

These issues and ideas can be found every week in local and international newspapers. A recent example is found in an article from *The Guardian* (2012) online, "Teenage Girl Wins a Seat in Uganda's Parliament":

> A teenage girl fresh out of high school has won a seat in Uganda's parliament . . . embarrassing some who say her success lowers expectations of lawmakers. . . . some critics say the position is too much responsibility for a young girl.

And why is the position "too much responsibility for a young girl?" Because she is a girl? Because she is 16 years old? Because she is not yet ready to do this work since she is (only) 16 years old? This is ageism—prejudice against a person or class of person based solely (or largely) on one characteristic or factor. She as a person is being judged (in)competent based on her chronological age, and maybe her "sex."

Seen here is a basic public conception of young people (and possibly, of sex, too, and in this case possibly of region, tribe, and family), and this idea and belief are targets for those who believe in the principles of and do civic youth work. In order that this not be the only way Ugandans see young people, Restless Development—a youth-led development agency with INGO (international nongovernmental organization) funds—advocates, in Uganda as its name suggests, for the active involvement of young people.

Another recent example comes from Russia, where news stories told about the Russian decision to ban non-Russian, outsider citizen groups (NGOs, voluntary associations, community-based organizations). It is these groups that have participated in working for political democracy. This is the home of youth civic engagement and civic youth work—working for democracy by cocreating with young people spaces for taking on and responding to issues of meaning and importance to them. These recent examples are neither atypical nor unique currently or historically. There have been and continue to be a wide diversity of groups supporting young people's civic and political engagement. What is common is that all challenge the local and global understandings of what it means to be and do a particular chronological age.

Conclusions

Civic youth work has been around as long as adults and youth have prepared young people to "play a role in their community" and nation. Here we name this practice and position it in the family of youth work. We name youth participation and youth engagement, youth activism, and the other family terms as citizen, citizenship, and lived citizen(ship). Here we call the worker who takes on the ethos, masters the skills, and embodies the practice a civic youth worker; and position this role, as mentioned, in the youth work family. By doing so, we make visible and available a basic approach to (healthy) youth development in the civic sphere: citizen (who is "young," typically 12–24 years old).

Doing this, we suggest that young people are systematically and largely (if not almost fully) marginalized, if not outright excluded, from everyday citizen work on issues meaningful and consequential to them, for others, and for a community. This is a plea to invite and support young people as citizens now (not citizens-becoming or future citizens), so that they can join (if they want) in working to sustain democracy and engage their and/or our collective issues and problems.

Reflective Questions

1. Is it both reasonable and useful to claim civic youth work as a "field of practice"?

2. Is "civic youth work" a good name for the field?
3. In what family of practice does civic youth work belong?
4. Is civic youth work as described so far a truly political practice?
5. What is the place of young people in civic youth work theory and practice?

Glossary

Civic apathy: Absence of care for neighborhood, community, or country; disinterest in being/acting as an active citizen

Craft orientation: The stance of a craft or field toward the work and toward the world beyond itself and its gaze—how the world is seen, ordered, interpreted, and responded to.

Gaze: Originally a psychoanalytical term and made popular by Jacques Lacan. It was later used by Michel Foucault to begin to describe how perception and experience often provide us with a way of seeing, and how some experiences and perceptions are given power over others, such as with medical doctors and diagnosis. In this text, we use it simply to describe a way of seeing: How one goes about noticing young people as having a political self.

Lived citizen(ship): Lived citizenship is a framing of youth civic engagement that places understanding of citizenship from the perspectives of education, politics, youth, and vocation. It is an attempt to get at civic engagement from inside—from the young person's embodied perspective and lived experience. Rather than focus on rights or responsibilities as basis for citizenship, the lived citizen understands citizenship as something that is personally experienced, a way of being.

Praxis: Describes action grounded in particular values. Based on Aristotle's writing praxis means: to act rightly and goodly; action that furthers human wellbeing. In critical pedagogy, based on the writing of Paulo Freire, it means reflection and action upon the world in order to change it. It is not merely doing something, which Freire refers to as activism, or simply talking about something, which Freire calls verbalism. Instead it refers to a creative and dialogical process, where people come together to describe and name their realities and then act with others to create a more non-violent, socially just, and inclusive society.

Tacit or implicit knowledge: The knowledge we have that we are unaware of, whose value to others we do not understand, and which, therefore, cannot be easily told to others. Teaching tacit or implicit knowledge requires extensive, personal contact between teacher and learner, and can often only be revealed through practice.

Youth work: A family of practices worldwide that support and deepen young people's knowledge, skill, and social, personal, and political development. Often grounded in educational philosophy and practice, including experiential, informal, critical, participatory, dialogic, and nonformal.

2

Contesting Youthhood:
Living Youth Citizen(ship)

Children are constructed as 'becoming' adults with political will rather than 'being' children without political voice. (Aitken, 2001, p. 23)

Youth civic engagement begins with an **image of the young person** (Friedman, 1988). Aitken (2001) accurately captured the dominant image we have of young people and citizenship in the United States: young people as becoming citizens rather than as being citizens. This raises questions: What are the consequences of this image for young people and for their democratic citizenship? Does this image fit with the stories young people tell about their involvement in civic and political work? Is this image of young people accurate, beneficial, or the opposite? To whom, when, why, and how? These questions often remain unanswered, as scholars and practitioners disagree over what is the conception of citizenship for which young people should be prepared: Is it the current type of civic and political involvement and civic engagement among young people? Is it best achieved by improved civics coursework, service learning, or other participatory approaches? These subjects are the substance of debates between and among scholars and practitioners, and these are often proxies for larger disagreements among practitioners and scholars as to who young people are and what they are capable of doing (and thinking). The different perspectives take for granted a particular understanding of a young person, and what a young person needs to become a true and full democratic citizen. Aitken (2001) cautioned us not to make our conclusions too quickly. The question for our society remains: Are young people becoming citizens or are they citizens already?

This question is at the base of every democratic, citizen-education initiative for young people, whether acknowledged or not. How we choose to answer this question has implications and consequences for youth, for citizenship, and for civic society, locally and nationally. This question leads us to the many different ways *child*, *young person*, and *young people* can be understood, and also to how these understandings, when coupled with arguments and evidence, shape our take on who a young person is, who young people are, and what their "needs" and wants are. Every image of youth has real-world consequences for actual young people, community, and others.

In the United States, the dominant image of young person and/or young people is a biophysiological developmental perspective (Crain, 1985; Lesko, 2001; Morss, 1990). This chapter begins with a brief summary of this perspective. This perspective is then placed in conversation with the constructivist perspective of young person, showing how this latter frame discloses a very different young person and an alternate way of understanding young people. These two understandings of young person/people are joined to different youth citizen(ship) conceptualizations. Then, the next section takes up citizen(ship), presents several definitions and meanings of this, and then works out the implications of each for youth people and their citizenship. Since both *youth* and *citizen* have often been defined conflictually, it is seen that the terms, ideas, and images *youth*, *citizen*, and *youth citizen* are all contested.

Recognizing *youth* and *citizen* as contested terms, the fourth section takes up the idea of "youth civic engagement," and begins to work out possible ways of understanding this. The meanings of *youth*, *citizen*, and *engagement* are put into conversation with empirical findings on youth civic engagement. Then, all of this is considered in relation to learning and education. The result is a basis for understanding the sociopolitical and youth development importance of civic youth work.

Conceptions of Young People

Young people, as such, are conceived of in a variety of ways, including what is seen on television, read about in the newspapers, our own experiences as young people, and our everyday encounters with young people, at least. Almost everyone has an idea of who "young people" are. This is true also in the literatures on youth civic engagement and youth citizenship (e.g., S. Bennett, 2000; Checkoway & Richards-Schuster, 2003). These ideas, representations, conceptions, meanings, and images of young person/people are not explicit; rather, these reveal themselves in the policies and resulting programs and other opportunities created for (not with or by) young people. For example, arguing for more traditional civic education makes explicit an image of young person as "deficient" and "unprepared" for citizenship. In contrast, providing opportunities for young people to work on issues they care about springs from a very different image of young person. Debates within the field of youth civic engagement, whether about citizenship rights for young people, participation opportunities, or civic literacy, are all based on particular, taken-for-granted images and ways of understanding and/or making sense of young people.

The dominant perspective used to understand young person in the United States is age-based development. The second is constructivist, described in the fields of sociology and anthropology (James, Jenks, & Prout, 1998). While there are many different conceptualizations of young people beyond these two, these serve to bring into question taken-for-granted assumptions and notions about young people, young person, and youth work.

The "eternal" young person: Developmental conception

Central to this perspective of young person is the idea that child, adolescent, or young person has a material existence (Jenks, 1996; Lesko, 2001; Mayall, 2002; Rogoff, 2003). Neither societies nor cultures are seen as having created the age roles of "child" and "adolescent"; rather these age categories are taken to be natural, as if special and separate categories of child and adolescent truly exist in the material world (not the conceptual world) as such. Young people are seen as eternal, in that they are believed to have always been present in the form we know and understand today, i.e., throughout historical time and across cultures (Rogoff, 2003). Developmentalists argue that this is true for any individual person of particular chronological age in any place and from any culture. Supporters of this image write about "the" three-year-old, or "the" teenager (Morss, 1990), claiming a universal and ahistorical understanding. To those who hold this view, race, gender, socioeconomic, political, and cultural characteristics are irrelevant. There is an essence of child or youth. These characteristics, factors, and variables have relatively little use for the understanding of young people and a young person. These simply influence the essence, but do not challenge its ontological status.

Biological metaphors best capture the "youth" idea within a **biophysiological developmental** frame. Humans are understood to be "growing." This is part of maturation. This perspective "uses elapsed time since birth as a measure of develop-ment" (Rogoff, 2003, p. 8). As young people age from child to adult, all pass through a series of ordered and structured universal stages, described as invariant, structured, and hierarchical (Crain, 1985). Change goes in one direction, is qual-itatively different across stages, with later stages being more complex than earlier stages. While recent concepts in development, such as "plasticity" and "bi-directionality," challenge age-stages, the image of adolescence as a preparatory stage for future maturation and development remains (Lerner & Steinberg, 2009). The goal of development is "adulthood."

These stages structure the process of becoming adults—a concept that is itself a social term and social construction, we argue below (Jenks, 1996; Mayall, 1994). From this perspective, our cognitive, social, and behavioral development is joined to our body's physical maturation. In this conception, all children of the same age tend to be similar, with common characteristics, patterns of behavior, and cogni-tive abilities; focus is on the young person, the individual. Typically omitted are all other influences on the biologically driven developmental process (Lansdown, 2005). The individual young person can be understood best if set apart from a social context, because this only confuses what is really going on in the young person. Such static makes it that more difficult to uncover universal truths about body-based maturation. "Age," as such, provides definition and gives meaning to developmen-tal stage. To know age is to know a person (Mayall, 1996). The individual person has little role in their development, with little to do with their own "growing up." This happens naturally. The person undergoes "specific processes," crises, and conflicts that produce "development"; and while results vary, the processes are the same for all children. Nancy Lesko (2001) has appropriately called this approach "biology as destiny" (p. 7). Biophysiological processes occur to persons. The exis-tential agency of the individual is greatly diminished.

This "universal path of development" is used to support the claims that adults are "developed" and that young people are in the "process of developing." Historically, development was understood as a **recapitulation process** (Lesko, 2001; Mayall, 1996). As a person changed from younger to older, from "infant," to "child," to "adolescent," and then to "adult," they also relived the historical stages, moving from uncivilized persons (children) to civilized persons (adults) (Lesko, 2001). Using such data, a person can be plotted on a line from infant to adult. Then, using research findings, appropriate responses can be given to the individ-ual's wants and needs. This is done by taking into account the person's stage of development, including the distance remaining to the finish line—full development or adulthood. "Directionality and progress are features inherent" in the developmental perspective, i.e., its telos (Morss, 1990, p.180). As such, this perspective details the ways young people are "lesser," "different," and "vulnerable," when compared to adults (Jenks, 1996). Recent research on the teen brain adds new metaphors such as, "all gas and no brakes," suggesting that young people are deficient and now a danger to themselves (and others?) (Payne, 2012). Young people in this conception are not quite ready for "real" life; they should be protected by (caring) adults.

To some, youth is the time process of preparing for "real life" (Wyn & White, 1997). Developmentally appropriate programming seeks to support young people's preparation for adult life by creating opportunities that match the youth's cognitive, social, and biological maturity (Meschke, Peter, & Bartholomae, 2012). When put together and compared to adults, youth are smaller, have less experience, and remain biologically, cognitively, and socially underdeveloped. For their own safety, and to ensure "healthy development," some argue, young people should be kept away from adult issues (e.g., political and community affairs) (Skelton & Valentine, 1998). To be appropriately included in the affairs of a community, young people should wait until they reach the "appropriate developmental stage." In this view, a person becomes "ready" for the "real world" when he or she has achieved the physical, cognitive, and social development of an adult.

Age binds person and physical maturation together and thus becomes the dominant way to understand person. This is seen in certain images of young people: inexperienced, naïve, innocent, lacking in the maturity necessary to make a serious and meaningful contribution to school, communities, and society. Within this perspective, it is easy to avoid considering the contribution children, adolescents, and young people could make to these, and it is easy to treat them and their concerns as frivolous and unimportant (Lesko, 2001). This perspective on young persons also provides "evidence" which has been used to keep young people out of public life. It is said that it is "in their best interests" to do so, because young people are not yet mature enough to participate, might be "hurt" physically or emotionally, and they might even "grow up too soon" (Jeffs, 2001). All of these images of young people, in the context of civic engagement, effectively remove them from public affairs and civic participation (Lesko, 2001; Mayall, 2002). But the developmental perspective is not the only way to understand young people. In contrast is the social-constructivist perspective, which conceptualizes young people as being actively involved in their own development, thus laying the foundation for their civic engagement. As will be shown, this image leads to active and participatory approaches to youth civic engagement.

"Constructing" the young person: Social-constructivist conception

Arguing against the overwhelming, dominant developmental view of the young person are practitioners and scholars of philosophy (Matthews, 1992; van Manen, 2002), psychology (Morss, 1990; Rogoff, 2003; Way, 1998), geography (Aitken, Lund, & Kjorholt, 2008; Ansell, 2005; Skelton & Valentine, 1998), sociology (Corsaro, 1997; James, Jenks, & Prout, 1998; Jenks, 1996), anthropology (Campbell, 2000; Danesi, 2003), cultural studies (Lesko, 2001; Nayak, 2003), youth work (Jeffs, 2001; VeLure Roholt, Baizerman, & Hildreth, 2013), and social work (Checkoway & Richards-Schuster, 2003), who understand young people as living within everyday social worlds. Young people "are cultural participants, living in a particular community at a specific time in history" (Rogoff, 2003, p. 10). They are always in-the-world(s). Understanding young person requires looking beyond the individual and recognizing that "who they are" is negotiated within social and cultural contexts (Aitken, 2001; Lesko, 2001; Mayall, 2002). To understand and describe young people requires describing and understanding the worlds they occupy and reside in. This perspective understands young people as connected and attached to others, and these relationships help craft "who they are" to us and how they come to be understood by themselves and others. The "constructed" young people perspective recognizes that young people are active members—agents—in their own processes of "growing up" (Pufall & Unsworth, 2004), and that our (adult) understanding of them is shaped by discourses used by both adults and young people to describe who young people are, what they do, and what they are able to do (Moss & Petrie, 2002; Tait, 2000). Our understanding is also shaped by the social institutions and social practices that serve to organize childhood, adolescence, and **youthhood** in contemporary times (Jenks, 1996; Stainton Rogers, 2004). Together these are what make them "young people." "Young person" is a social category of time passing—i.e., age—socially constructed out of social expectations and from normative thought, feeling, and action socially named and culturally meaningful.

This perspective highlights the importance of place, history, economics, politics, culture, community, and family for defining who young people are and how to understand them. Being-in-the-world means, in this view, that a person cannot be understood outside of the context he or she lives in. Young people are not "eternal," but rather "cultural" and historical (Rogoff, 2003). What it means to be a person of a particular age, shape, or size is determined in part by how those around the individual person make sense of these. These same contexts define behavior, actions, or activities for young people as acceptable or unacceptable: context matters deeply (Goncu, 1999). Who young people are is connected to the ways their everyday lives are organized and ordered—often by processes far away from individual, family, or community (Suárez-Orozco & Qin-Hilliard, 2004), and also by the meaning assigned to young people's actions. Rather than being a universal, a single category, young person as role in this perspective is seen as having many possibilities. **Youth** is a plural rather than a unified category (Moss & Petrie, 2002). What this means is that there are in life many (types of) youth, many ways "youth" can be done, and many ways one can do and be "youth." This perspective highlights the interactive construction of what it means to be a young person, demonstrating both how the young person actively participates in this construction, and is limited by the ways others talk about people of particular ages, and by proximate and distal social arrangements.

In these contexts young persons actively cocreate, craft their worlds and themselves. They have "agency" (Mayall, 2002). A young person is seen as actively making choices and engaging in activities that shape who he or she is, because a person is both shaped by, as well as helps to shape, his or her everyday world (Lincoln & Guba, 1985). Through participating in daily activities, young people craft and construct knowledge about self, community, and world. It is this engagement in everyday, ordinary activities, and the meanings they and others make of these, that create what it means to be "child," or "youth" (Gubrium, Holstein, & Buckholdt, 1994). In many ways, they accomplish "youth": young person as such is one accomplishment, as is teenage girl, skater, goth, and citizen. That is what it means "to be a young person around here, now" (Baizerman, 1998). These are interpretative, not universal categories, with the characteristics of each jointly determined by young people in their interactions with others: by media, in families, and in communities (Mayall, 1994). Youth as a social category is socially constructed. Categories teach about what to expect from individual members, and we see individuals through the images and expectations of the category.

Being situated in worlds also means that the world influences and shapes the young person. Especially important to the construction of the category, "young person," are the ways in which young people are described, talked about, or referred to within particular contexts. The discourses we use to name and "talk about" young people have real-world consequences for them and for us, in turn (Moss & Petrie, 2002; Tait, 2000). How teachers, parents, and others talk about young people shapes who and what youth are taken to be, what they can do, and how this is assessed (Lesko, 2001). "Child" or "youth" does not exist in the everyday world, but comes into existence through the language used to describe people of this age; the "child is made present through a variety of forms of discourse" (Jenks, 1996, p. 32). These ways of naming young people are what "provides the spaces and times for people to enact [the social ways of] childhoods as locally defined" (Mayall, 2002, p. 23). All of this has practical consequences for young people, a young person, for others, and for community. For example, teachers talk about students, and police often talk about working with juveniles (delinquents). Each of these terms carries social expectations, at least by the adults, and these guide how they talk to young people they meet, even if they are incomplete understandings of young people (Gubrium, Holstein, & Buckholdt, 1994). Rarely are young people only students or juveniles. These same people may also be community activists, caregivers of younger siblings, elderly parents or grandparents, and household income earners. These ways of understanding young people remain invisible, if not found, noticed, and named. Young person as a category is brought into existence, definition, and meaning through the discourses used to talk about them.

This social-constructivist perspective also illuminates the ways in which social institutions, generational structures, and policies and practices promoted within communities have real consequences for particular youthhoods over other ways of doing and being youth. How youthhood and adolescence are socially organized does not happen serendipitously or by biology and/or accident. It is by age and "generational structures," and how these are supported by policies and practices that organize that age category called youth(hood) (Mayall, 2002). The ways professionals (teachers, youth workers, psychologists, social workers, juvenile corrections, etc.) practice, and how organizations support these practices, work to create and maintain particular realities for young people, and these shape what young people are allowed to do and be (Gubrium, Holstein, & Buckholdt, 1994). These social, political, economic, and related structures appear in the world as "facts" which are typical and independent of individual will (Jenks, 1996). Practically, this means that other ways of doing and being youth are less important, less "normal," less "appropriate." From this perspective, the current possibilities of being and doing young person within a particular world in time and/or place are contested (Aitken, 2001). This is where youth civic engagement comes in. We are working our way toward this field and focus.

Connecting citizen(ship) to conception of young person

In a developmental perspective, the idea of young people as citizens now is rare. Instead, focus is on them as citizens-in-training (yet none is offered, usually). The population's deficiencies, what needs should be worked out, whether "ability" or skill, shapes what opportunities (if any) young people are provided. In contrast, in a constructivist perspective, young people are taken as "citizens now." This image of young person supports innovative, participatory, and active citizen opportunities and educational offerings. Participation is seen as educational (Lave & Wenger, 1991), and through inviting and supporting young people's community contributions, young people also learn and master the citizen role.

These two distinct and opposite conceptualizations of young person make clear the little agreement on who and what young people are, or how we should understand the idea, "youth," and the individual young person. Biology is read as "age," and this may be a factor in influencing who the young person is and what he or she can do. But age as such is not the only factor (Aitken, 2001). Other factors include the way young people are responded to by youth policies and the accepted practices of working with them, as well as by the opportunities made available to youth. All of these play significant parts in determining what and/or who is "young people" in this place, at this time (Goncu, 1999). Tension between these different conceptions of youth has profound consequences for actual young people within actual youth civic engagement programmatic initiatives. How one talks about young people often provides the answer to the question: Are they citizen-becoming or are they already citizens?

Youth and Citizen

Being citizens or living in "citizen ways" (citizen(ship) or lived-citizen) (VeLure Roholt, Hildreth, & Baizerman, 2008) is always a possibility for individuals (when permitted). However, it is more difficult to fit this into the category, youth, and for the youth population precisely because, in one of the images and perspectives (developmental), young people simply are not able to do this. While, in the other view (constructivist), any actual young person may be able to do and be citizen. How young people as image, category, population, and individuals are understood and responded to either opens or closes the doors and pathways available to young people who want to "make a difference" (as a citizen, as an activist) on an issue meaningful and consequential to them, and to others (James, 2011). This is how image, perspective, and theoretical orientation touch actual opportunities for actual young people. Youth civic engagement can take its stand with the constructivist view, without denying the biochemical, physiological, and other findings on adolescents and adolescence by those working in the developmental science tradition. Within this constructivist perspective of a young person, youth civic engagement is about testing in real conditions whether this particular group of individuals or youth can do and be citizens. This brings us to the question: What is democratic citizenship?

What is democratic citizenship?

Citizenship has been understood variously throughout Western/Northern and other histories, and it remains widely used, but without agreement in meaning. It is a **contested concept** (Gorham, 1992; Haste, 2010). Not every citizenship scholar would agree with Gorham (1992), and their very disagreement only adds to the idea that citizenship is contested. Here, by examining competing definitions and understandings of citizenship, we provide another basic view on the youth citizen. We do not provide a full or deep analysis of different conceptions, but rather a general overview of competing views and the understandings which follow from each. This is a way into the topics of youth civic engagement and civic youth work.

Current conceptions of democratic citizenship begin with T. H. Marshall's (1950) emphasis on individual rights in civil, political, and social arenas. In his view, citizens are those who recognize rights guaranteed under law and act accordingly. This rights-based definition is criticized by those holding a communitarian conception of citizenship, which emphasizes the individual's communal responsibility. Citizens are those who understand their community responsibilities and act accordingly. These two ways of seeing citizen have been increasingly scrutinized, especially in the context of citizenship as a contested concept.

Attempts at defining or getting at the core meaning of democratic citizenship often flounder for at least two reasons. One is Gorham's (1992) contention that a common definition of citizen is bound to fail in the United States, and in other developed democracies, because of the diverse ways it can be and is exercised. While everyone might agree that being a good citizen "means to be independent, politically active, politically aware, and engaged in the issues of the community" (Gorham, 1992, p. 12), the meaning of these values in practice is much more difficult to get at. For example, many youth civic engagement studies focus on young people's intention to vote, without considering possible intended political meanings by those who choose not to vote (Amna & Zetterberg, 2010). Choosing not to vote does not always mean that one is a poor democratic citizen. A person might believe that the election is rigged, or that with only one candidate running for office, one's vote does not matter, or it may be simply that their experience of living in the country does not connect to the espoused ideas of living in a free, just, and fair society (Rubin, 2007).

Other conceptions fail to acknowledge that citizenship is much more than rights or responsibilities. Storrie (2004) argued that "citizenship is primarily a specific cultural achievement" (p. 57), the primary task of which is to "maintain and enhance this cultural achievement" (Storrie, 2004, p. 57). Citizenship, in this view, is produced through our actions. This is true, too, for new rights and responsibilities which must be created. A concise definition of citizen(ship) does not get at what it means to an individual, a group, and a population to be a citizen (Gorham, 1992).

Indeed, democratic citizenship remains looser, more open, freer when not defined. Without agreed upon conceptions or meaning, each of us must decide what democratic citizenship means for our generation, and in this way, further reinforce the idea that citizenship is what each of us must accomplish throughout our lives. This notion has real potency for youth citizens(ship). Do opportunities exist for young people to accomplish democratic citizenship?

All of these scholars agree that democratic societies depend on successive generations developing the necessary knowledge, skills, and attitudes to sustain and recreate the basic structures of democratic life (Dahl, 1998). Basic to this is ensuring spaces where these can be tried on and accomplished by successive generations. Historically, this has been a concern for civic educators. While some disagreement continues on what specific knowledge, skills, and attitudes are required for democratic citizenship, all agree that flourishing democracies depend at least on citizens attaining **civic literacy** (e.g., Butts, 1980; Chilcoat & Ligon, 2001; Patrick, 2000), understanding of democratic structures and ways of living and being democratic.

Civic literacy goes beyond our specific content to include ways of coming to know and figuring out how to act democratically in specific contexts, learning both content and process. This fits with the notion of "action competence," a state of readiness to participate meaningfully within particular contexts (Holden & Clough, 1998, p. 18). Examples of such contexts may include school, community center, community, and nation. Civic literacy means having the ability to do "social inquiry" and cocreate with others appropriate responses to what is learned (Dewey, 1927, p. 167). It means to have understanding and competence in using society's symbols, in going about figuring out what these might mean for self, others, and society, now and in the future. Young people are said to have little civic literacy. This may be because their only exposure to it is in school civics classes, and they have a poor teacher. They are kept from experiences during which they could master civic literacy. Their limited knowledge here is then used to argue why they are not yet citizens.

Why young people are not accepted as citizens

By most reports, young people are not yet civically literate (S. Bennett, 2000; Utter, 2011), although recent scholarship has begun to contest this conclusion (Sloam,

2012). It is based on large survey data about how well young people have mastered democratic civic knowledge, skills, and "dispositions." Without these, it is believed that young people are unable to participate in democratic society (Wichowsky, 2002), making these results even more alarming for educators, political scientists, and policy-makers. Such surveys reinforce the idea that young people are not yet ready to be or even able to be democratic citizens. This fits the developmental way of understanding young person.

Of the many surveys and tests measuring young people's civic knowledge, skills, and dispositions, three are commonly cited as evidence that young people do not have adequate preparation for democratic citizenship. First, young people score poorly when asked to recall key facts of American history and government (Gallup & Gallup, 2000). Scholars cite these findings as evidence that most young people do not receive an adequate historical education about the United States. This, they argue makes young people unprepared for citizenship. Troublesome is the fact that they disagree as to what would be adequate historical content (Hirsch, 1999; Marciano, 1997; Ravitch, 2002). Second, international studies on young people's voting behavior find that they choose not to participate in large numbers in national or local elections (Thau & Eisinger, 2000; Utter, 2011), with exceptions, of course, as in the U.S. presidential elections in 2008 and 2012 (Circle, n.d.). This is taken to mean that young people do not understand the primary responsibilities of democratic citizenship—voting. Finally, studies find that a majority of young people ignore political affairs and traditional news media. This raises concern that they are "apathetic" and cynical (Mattson, 2003; Moore, 2003). Scholars (e.g., Bennett, 2000; Circle, 2003; Utter, 2011) have interpreted these findings to suggest that young people do not have the basic civic literacy necessary for appropriate civic participation. (Do most adults, by these standards?)

Citizenship, as such, comes to be clearly defined by looking at what such scholars determine that young people lack or need. For scholars, citizenship means: voting or intent to vote, knowledge of key historical and governmental facts, and attentiveness to current affairs. This conception supports the conclusion that young people are "unprepared" to be democratic citizens. What should be done to rectify this? More appropriate preparation. These studies portray young people as deficient in citizenship knowledge, values, and action. This fits with the common perceptions of young people as "not yet" ready or capable, of youth as a time for "preparation," and of youth as not adult where adults are (supposed to be).

This way of understanding citizenship ignores the diverse ways people of all ages accomplish democratic citizen; it also raises further troubling questions: Are citizens only those who can recall key, country-specific, historical and government facts? Are citizens only those who vote in local, state, and national elections? Are citizens only those who are not apathetic or cynical? These are not the criteria used to judge citizenship for adults. Why are these used for young people? Adults can be citizens regardless of their voting behavior, their ability to recall key facts, or how well they keep up with current affairs. How is it that similar data on adults are not interpreted the same way, as a challenge to their citizen status? For adults, the alternative interpretation is that the citizenry is uninformed (Delli Carpini & Keeter, 1989). To use a single factor to decide whether or not adults are citizens or are unprepared for citizenship seems outrageous (except gender, race, social class, and language!). Citizenship is a complex social status and process. Yet when these same topics are studied with young people, it is acceptable that data are used to argue that young people are not ready for citizen rights or responsibilities. Their citizen status is brought into question because of their chronological age, and how prevailing images and perceptions of youth make sense of age as such, of youth as such, and of youth as citizens. These images are interpretative frames. Used as such, these have political consequences, regardless of political intentions.

Single variable and some multiple variable analyses also are interpreted within a narrow frame. For example, youth cynicism has a prominent place in the literature on youth civic engagement (Bennett, 1997, 2000; Fowler, 1990; Putnam, 1995). In these accounts, it is difficult to separate cynicism from "indifference," or "boredom." Duffy (2000) reminded us that cynicism does not mean that young people are disinterested. Rather, cynicism may indicate a degree of engagement; it is hard to be cynical if one never pays attention to what is going on. One could make similar arguments about voting and about "apathy." What statement do some young people intend to and believe they are making when they choose not to vote? First, is this a choice, or has the political system kept them from registering or has not tried to register them? These questions illuminate alternative interpretations of the findings on youth civic engagement ,and suggest alternative recommendations (see Byrne Fields, n.d.). Seen here is how research strategy, design, and interpretation transform the very basic, complex notion of citizen(ship) into an age-graded, single-variable conception, thereby distorting the very idea and its practice.

There are other conceptions of youth citizenship. These are based on researchers' everyday experience with young people in a variety of settings. In one study on community-building efforts, Finn and Checkoway (1998) described the many ways young people contribute to their communities, showing that they do this prior to any specific preparation (by adults). "Working to contribute" is the preparation to learn how to contribute; they learn by doing (Foley, 1999) and through participating (Lave & Wenger, 1991). This study agrees with comments made almost two decades earlier in the United Kingdom by the renowned Mark Smith (1982), who argued that young people are "creators," and that they have the ability to contribute significantly to their communities, if only we allow them to do so. In agreement with these conceptions by his colleague, Tony Jeffs (2001) argued that such opportunities can only be made available by providing young people with the rights adults take for granted, particularly the ability to participate in society as citizens. These British perspectives challenge current understandings of young people and citizenship, here and in many places worldwide.

Up to this point, we have illustrated the contested understandings of "young people" and "citizenship." These are not simple terms with tight definitions; rather these terms are given diverse meanings, many of which contradict or challenge each other. In this they are a Wittgensteinian "family of resemblances" (Manser, 1967), of meanings. While this way of understanding these concepts is acknowledged in theoretical and empirical studies of young people and of democratic citizenship, much of this is forgotten when the two are joined in studies of young people's citizenship. These hold to a narrow understanding of both elements—young people and citizenship—although change is beginning (Lansdown, 2005; Weller, 2007). The young person in image, civic practice, and scholarship, remains deficient, and citizenship is still treated as a discrete set of knowledge, skills, and dispositions. This view is challenged by the youth citizen perspective.

Youth Citizen

Our analysis leads to a focal question: How might citizenship be described and/or defined so as to include young people? In recent years, much effort has been given to understanding young people as citizens. Leading these efforts are scholars studying young people's participation in a variety of contexts (e.g., Checkoway & Richards-Schuster, 2003; Finn & Checkoway, 1998; Hart, 1992; Jeffs, 2001; Sabo, 2003), and political theorists who argue for a broad understanding of citizenship (Boyte, 1991; Boyte & Farr, 1997; Gorham, 1992; Jeffs, 2001). These authors provide new understandings of young people citizen(ship). They support the idea of young people as democratic citizen—youth citizenship. These theories and studies provide evidence that what is taken to be basic to adult citizenship (voting, attentiveness to adult issues, etc.) does not provide good guidance for understanding young people's democratic citizenship. And these scholars challenge the typically unstated assumption that adult citizenship is the desired goal, the only example to follow, or the standard of measure. Two examples of this alternative perspective are presented: the theory of public work, and Roger Hart's model of youth participation. These perspectives provide new understandings of young people and the youth citizen, supporting the idea of young people as democratic citizens—youth citizen(ship).

Public work

Youth citizenship is possible when citizen means more than voting, recalling key facts of a country's history and government, and/or attentiveness to current public affairs. "Public work" provides an enlarged understanding of citizenship, one that makes it possible for young people to be read and accepted as citizens. Boyte and Farr (1997) defined "public work" as "the expenditure of visible efforts by ordinary citizens whose collective labors produce things or create processes of lasting civic value" (p. 42). Public work is part of what a citizen does. The theory of public work provides support for the youth citizen through an emphasis on a small group or a public focus of the individual and collective work. That is, one's everyday activities can be citizen work, i.e., citizenship develops over time, is skill-based, and requires learning.

Public work challenges the idea that citizen is necessarily an individual status and act. Public work changes the focus from individual to group and away from what an individual must know to be a democratic citizen. Drawing on historical movements in the United States, Boyte (1991) asserted that public work is done by groups of citizens. When engaged in public work, people "work on concrete issues of mutual concern" (Boyte & Skelton, 1997, p. 16). In public work, a group is responsible for getting the work done. This has important implications for youth citizens. Public work as an idea allows citizens to be seen as people with varying levels of knowledge, skills, and dispositions who together accomplish joint goals and objectives. These everyday activities are the stuff of citizen(ship) and the "political."

Public work argues for a Deweyan (Dewey, 1927) understanding of politics. In this conception politics is "the public work of problem-solving" (Boyte, 1991, p. 765). Politics is the work done nationwide in communities every day. By arguing for this vision of politics and citizenship, a new standard is set: everyone can do it. "Engaging in politics" is what we all do over the course of our lives, although many of us may never interpret these actions as "political." When we notice a public problem and work with others to respond, we are engaging in politics and being political. Missing in everyday language and interpretation is the meaning of this work as political; typically this work is not read as political. Public work emphasizes "mapping the political and civic dimensions in different settings" throughout everyday activities (Boyte, 1991, p. 765). Public work is a strategy which repositions politics and citizenship. For democracy to flourish, everyday public work as political is basic. For understanding democracy the notion of public work is basic. Democratic citizenship in this view does not depend on age or knowledge, but instead on the meanings given to everyday activities. Citizens are those who recognize that their everyday actions are political, and who interpret these as such in a political hermeneutic. Certainly, this is possible for young people, as well as adults.

Public work as an interpretation can be used to support the youth citizen by describing citizenship as a location, a site, for learning about democracy, governance, and politics. In this view, individuals engaged in problem-solving do not necessarily come with the knowledge, skills, or dispositions required for addressing the problem. Rather, these result from participating in this work (Boyte, 1995). We become citizens by engaging in public work, not by knowing particular knowledge, mastering specific skills, or embodying definitive dispositions. Citizenship is far too dynamic. By locating citizenship in the everyday work done "by the people, for the people," it follows that each new generation will have to learn and know different knowledge and skills because these are needed to confront each (new) problem. Citizenship, in this view, is "continually developed over time" and "requires practice" (Center for Democracy and Citizenship, 2001). By debunking the idea that citizenship refers to the mastery of specific knowledge, skills, and dispositions, public work makes citizenship as sociopolitical and sociolegal statuses accessible to all, youth included. Emphasized above all is participation: we become citizens through participating in public (i.e., collective) work.

Youth participation

Recognizing citizenship as participating in public work requires a deeper understanding of participation. Roger Hart's (1992) "ladder of participation" has become valuable for recognizing the difference between nonparticipation and participation. When placed together with the theory and model of public work, one can clarify the notion of the youth citizen. Hart's (1992) model distinguished nonparticipation from participation by the degree of voice, choice, transparency, and information in "participatory" programs for young people.

Table 2.1. Distinguishing between Participation and Non-Participation

	Participation	Non-Participation
Voice	Young people are able and encouraged to express personal opinions and thoughts and these shape the joint work that is done.	Young people are used to express the ideas and opinions of adults. Their opinion is secondary.
Choice	Young people have the opportunity to participate in many different ways and can choose which of these is best for them.	Young people are not asked to participate but are told.
Transparency	Structures for young people's participation are explicit and open for review. Young people's participation role is clear, as is adults'.	Structures for young people's participation are implicit and not discussed. Young people's participation role is unclear, and adults' role is denied.
Information	Young people know both the why and the what of their participation.	Young people are simply told what to do.

The idea of "voice," especially in reference to children and youth, has received a great deal of attention (e.g., Lansdown, 2005; Pufall & Unsworth, 2004). For Hart, voice refers to young people being allowed to form and state their own opinions and thoughts (Hart, 1999). Participatory experiences are those that encourage and provide young people with the support required for them to get involved. To Hart (1999), nonparticipatory initiatives are those where adults use young people to "carry" their own messages to others (p. 40), while participation is found in efforts that allow young people to discuss issues they find important, and to formulate their own opinions, even if participating adults disagree. To those familiar with the United Nations Convention on the Rights of the Child, voice has a particular ring, as do the other categories of this model.

In this model, choice is a distinguishing feature of participatory efforts. Participatory initiatives are those that "maximize the opportunity for any child to choose to participate at the highest level of their ability" (Hart, 1999, p. 42). Fully participatory initiatives are those that allow young people to decide how they want to participate, and do not equate this choice as their "failing to live up to their potential" or "overextending" themselves. Instead, young people are welcomed and supported to participate as they wish. Participatory efforts also are those that make the structure of participation explicit and open for negotiation; they are transparent. This requires that young people be told who made the decision about their involvement and why, and be notified of any limitations on their decision-making (Hart, 1999). Fully participatory programs are full of information. Their participation is based on knowing about the issue they are working on and how they are being asked to work on it.

Within these general principles, Hart described eight different levels of participation. The first three refer to what he called nonparticipation and include: manipulation, decoration, and tokenism (Hart, 1992). The other five rungs describe participatory approaches to working with young people, including: assigned but informed; consulted and informed; adult-initiated, shared decisions with children; child-initiated and directed; and child-initiated, shared decisions with adults (Hart, 1992; See Table 2.2).

Table 2.2. Hart's Ladder of Participation

Rung	Description
1	Manipulation
2	Decoration
3	Tokenism
4	Assigned but Informed
5	Consulted and Informed
6	Adult-initiated, shared decisions with children
7	Child-initiated and directed
8	Child-initiated, shared decisions with adults

While some have criticized this model of participation as adult-centered (see John, 2003), we think that it provides a useful way for understanding young people's participation. What makes Hart's work important is recognizing that participation is not dichotomous, but diverse in type, style, authenticity, and the like. The ladder of participation opens up possibilities for young people to be participants in different ways. This is important for the youth citizen in that how young people participate in public work can be quite varied, as long as it continues to be true participation. It opens up the possibility for young people of different abilities to be (seen as) citizens. Let us now combine this discussion of participation with the earlier one on public work.

Combining youth participation and public work

What is it about active participation in public work that provides young people the possibility to be, to be seen as, and to be accepted as citizens? In this view, citizen is a role and identity for young people who work (participate) together in authentic and meaningful ways on public issues important to them.

These two components—participation and public work—can be used to make a compelling argument for transforming the way citizenship and young people are understood. Used together they provide a clear framework for initiatives that encourage young people to be and to perform the roles of democratic citizens. Yet, resistance continues to the notion of seeing young people as citizens. This may result from adult realization of how much they have to change if young people are to be invited and supported as citizens—in these roles and with this identity. The participation of youth may be perceived as a threat to established power relations between adults and young people (John, 2003; Malone & Hartung, 2010). If young people are to become citizens, adults are in a position to make this difficult. It may be easier to get support for some notion of youth as participant than for the notion of youth as citizen, when this includes young people's voice, choice, and participation in decision-making, as well as group action.

To accept this latter view requires that young people be invited, encouraged, and supported in acting in ways many adults will find uncomfortable, even disrespectful. It is as if young people can have a voice as long as it agrees with adult opinion (e.g., John, 2003; Lee, 2001). Young people can (be allowed to) make choices, as long as these are "good" ones, from an adult perspective. Adults want young people to learn how to make decisions, as long as they do not disagree with them or argue against them. And we want young people to act as long as they do what we want them to do. The issues here, in terms of cross-age and intergenerational relations, are about power, position, and feelings; about history, philosophy, and culture. Clearly, all of this is not simply about age as such.

Youth citizenship depends on more than young people's choices and actions. As Louise Chawla (2002) discovered in her work with young people worldwide, children often lack the latent political power that most adults take for granted:

> Although they may learn, through adult-initiated examples of participation, how to move to child-initiated projects, when the time comes to implement their ideas they will still need adults who will stand beside them and ensure they are treated with respect (p. 235).

Young people's citizenship, in the U.S., depends on adults' willingness to allow young people to act as democratic citizens, and on adult designation of where young people are allowed to use their voice, make choices and decisions, and take action (Gorham, 1992). Voice, choice, decision-making, and action are youth civic engagement.

Youth Civic Engagement

We argued that youth civic engagement cannot be understood without first examining two key terms—*youth* and *citizen*. This we did, and found both to be contested, with multiple meanings. These multiple meanings are also found in the multiple approaches and efforts designed to enhance youth civic engagement. Such efforts have the same purpose: to increase the likelihood that young people will continue to be citizens over their life course, that they will act as democratic citizens by participating in political and community groups, voting and paying attention to political issues. Gibson (2001) described four main approaches to enhancing youth civic engagement: civic education, service-learning, social/community change, and youth development. While workers in each school of youth civic engagement may disagree on who young people are and their conception of democratic citizen, all have in common the aim of engaging young people in democratic practice. These differences in approach are pedagogical.

Historically, the education of young people for citizenship has been grounded in one or more of these approaches (Gibson, 2001). For example, a political science classroom teacher may present a detailed history of the U.S. government, and the role and activities of various governmental branches. To complement this material, students may be asked to do service work in the community, or they may be given school credit for participating in a political campaign or sitting on a community committee. In civic education, combining two or three of these approaches is not uncommon (Butts, 1980; Dynneson & Gross, 1991; Farquhar & Dawson, 1979; Meier, Cleary, & Davis, 1952; Patrick, 1967; Thurston, 1947).

This is true also for service-learning, which is listed here as a single type of youth civic engagement. Although Gibson (2001) disagreed, service-learning can include a number of civic engagement models, including: service provision, social/community change, and youth development activities, depending on how the service-learning is organized and facilitated, i.e., depending on the host organization and the youth worker. Separating the four approaches analytically should not be confused with how things work in the world, where the four can be mixed, in whole or in part. Table 2.3 is an overview of the four approaches to enhancing young people's civic engagement (Based on Gibson, 2001 and Boyte & Kari, n.d.).

Table 2.3. Overview of Youth Civic Engagement Approaches

Youth Civic Engagement Type	How to Understand Engagement?	Who are Citizens?	Who are Young People?
Civic Education	Providing a "back to the basics" education, emphasizing founding documents and history of US.	Individuals educated on politics and government.	Individuals who have not received sufficient education on politics and government.
Providing Service to Others	Helping their communities and those in need.	Community caregivers.	Becoming community caregivers.
Social/ Community Change	Participating in political and social action.	Change agents.	Potential problem solvers.
Individual Development	Participating in extracurricular activities.	Individuals with a developed civic identity.	Individuals in the process of developing a civic identity.

These four approaches can be found at the root of youth services worldwide; these are now international practices. Next, we look more closely at each of these approaches, provide an example from its literature, and discuss what research has shown to be its link to youth citizen development.

Civic education

Civic education received renewed interest in the George W. Bush administration, with calls for a national civics curriculum (Milbank, 2002). This is the traditional approach to citizen education. Proponents argue that young people will become democratic citizens through a thorough examination of our country's history, political institutions and processes, and significant cultural stories (Butts, 1980; Ravitch, 1997). The focus is on facts, concepts, and generalizations from a wide range of social sciences, as these help students understand the formation and continuation of national governmental systems (Butts, 1980; Moore, 2003). Such education, it is argued, can be achieved best by reorganizing public-school curricula and requiring coursework. One particularly vocal group in the US argues for a national, standardized curriculum that focuses on American history and culture, and removes current foci on bilingualism and multiculturalism (Hirsch, 1997; Ravitch, 1997, 2002). Other variations of this approach include a common concern for uniformity—the use of the same curriculum nationwide. There are many examples of how this approach is being implemented.

Zeiser (2001) presented one example based on this civics approach, the curriculum initiative, "Building Better Citizens," cosponsored by the University of North Florida's Institute of Government and Girls Incorporated of Jacksonville, Florida. This program seeks to increase participants' "knowledge of local, state, and federal government, motivate them to become involved in community issues and needs; and build an understanding of what it means to be a responsible citizen" (Zeiser, 2001, p. 290). Classroom activities include lectures, guest speakers from local nonprofit organizations, research on public issues, a mock presidential election, and the keeping of personal journals. Experiential activities were included, such as visiting political party headquarters, city hall, and volunteering at a homeless shelter. The focus is on presenting and describing the workings of the United States government, both local and national, along with the skills and attitudes required to successfully participate as citizens in U.S. political processes at all levels.

Studies on the results of such approaches provide mixed findings. Niemi and Junn (1998) found that such approaches increase participants' knowledge of government and politics and improve their reasoning on civic matters. Further, they discussed the possibility that these types of approaches lead to more and more refined political attitudes; civic education can positively influence young people's political attitudes, they asserted. In another study, Corbett (1991) found less promising results, and concluded that these courses are not very effective in transmitting knowledge or political attitudes. There may be some truth in each of these findings.

Niemi and Junn (1998) studied the effect of various classroom practices on learning civic content. They found that discussion and analysis of the material and the use of current events positively contributed to an increased understanding of civic matters. It is possible that Corbett's (1991) study focused on courses where the main classroom activity consisted of memorization and frequent testing, two practices that Niemi and Junn found to hinder student learning. Also possible in the eight years between the two studies is that school practices may have changed significantly, thus contributing to the inconsistent findings. (Note: At the present time (2013), we wonder, what is the shelf life of such studies?)

While classroom instruction might lead to more and more refined political attitudes among students, it may have little effect on how people act in their communities. Jeffs (2001) reported studies (Jennings, Langton, & Niemi, 1974; Russell, 1950) that found little evidence to link civic learning in schools to political behavior in the community because, he argued, schools often forget that democracy is more than a governmental system, it is a way of life. For schools to support democratic learning, they must themselves be democratically structured and must support teachers and administrators behaving in ways supportive of "associational living" (Dewey, 1916). Possibly missing is a congruence between what is taught and what is lived.

Providing service

Service is a second of the four approaches to youth civic engagement. It includes both volunteering and some forms of service-learning. Here particular value is placed on young people's doing actual work in a community. The argument is that provision of service to others can be the foundation of citizenship (Bass, 1997; McLellan & Youniss, 2003; Terry & Bohnenberger, 2003). Implementing this approach, some schools require students to complete a certain number of volunteer hours, while others encourage students to become involved in volunteer activities through either elective or compulsory coursework. The focus here is on the needs of the community, with students asked to fulfill a "need" already defined by the community, one that benefits the community (Billig, 2000; Waterman, 1997). Young people provide "service" to the community by working "there"; typically outside of a school building. In this approach, a community organization defines both role and activity for students, as well as the community issue or concern they will work on. Students come to the community and take on these already defined roles, and do already decided tasks. In service-learning, all of this is incorporated into a school course, showing here the difference between volunteer service and service-learning (Waterman, 1997). In this approach, programs seek to balance service to community and classroom academic learning (Eyler & Giles, 1999), providing an opportunity to combine the action with reading and teacher-guided reflection. It is clear how this is school-friendly, and friendly, too, to typical school pedagogies: It fits the rigid school schedule, is attached to formal curriculum, can meet curricular and/or learning outcomes, and is teacher-directed and controlled—for learning, safety, liability, and the like. Service-learning is a school-friendly approach.

Youniss and Yates's (1997) study of a service-learning/social justice class provided a detailed example. It began with an academic course—here, a social justice course at a Catholic high school. The course curriculum focused on a variety of issues, including: homelessness, poverty, immigrant issues and abuses, urban violence, and capital punishment. An examination of Catholic moral philosophy and a review of the biographies of major figures in social justice struggles provided additional course foci. All of these were combined with a weekly community-service experience at a homeless shelter, where students prepared and served a meal and cleaned up. Classroom activity included reflecting on the service experience, and linking it to course readings and class discussions. For example, after reading a passage from Teilhard de Chardin, students would be asked if they thought their actions "helped to move humanity forward or backward" (Youniss & Yates, 1997). Service-learning seeks to make pedagogical the service experience to enrich and deepen students' understanding of what they are learning in and because of their doing, as well as how to join reflection to action.

Studies on service-learning and volunteering often explore how well these approaches enhance young people's civic skills, knowledge, and attitudes. Studies on service-learning have shown that students who participate in formal service-learning projects have a deeper understanding of the subject matter, remember more of it, and use it outside of class (Eyler & Giles, 1999). Studies done by Richard Battistoni (2000) found service-learning a potent civic educator when accompanied by proper preparation and reflection. In earlier studies (1997) he also found service-learning to be an effective way to educate about diversity and to improve students' communication abilities. Further, Billig (2000) argued that service-learning increases a student's feelings of civic and social responsibility and political effectiveness. Youniss and Yates (1997) found that participation in service-learning can help young people form political identities, increase their awareness of political issues, and enhance a desire to continue doing community service. What service-learning does not do well is improve young people's political knowledge, or increase the amount of time they attend to political affairs in the press, nor does it support learning transfer to other life domains (Hunter & Brisbin, 2000). This latter point is critical theoretically and for evaluation (Chapter Six). Also contested in the literature is the idea that service-learning promotes civic responsibility. Hepburn, Niemi, and Chapman (2000) highlighted a study in which service-learning students did not perceive an association between their service and civic responsibility. Looking at all these data, it is not at all clear whether service-learning enhances the civic engagement of young people, and if it does, in what realms and with what personal and other consequences—also topics for evaluation.

These mixed findings will not surprise those who organize service-learning. This may be because service-learning has become topical (Reiman, Sprinthall, & Thies-Sprinthall, 1999) and common practice for schools and community youth organizations, and this has led to service-learning courses which do not always meet "best practices." For example, it is known that the quality of the student experience improves when there are high-quality and diverse field service placements, when ongoing and regular, guided reflection has been rigorously planned, where the classroom includes a diversity of students, and where students participate over an extended time (Eyler & Giles, 1999). "The key success is likely to be found in the nature of the service experience and how well the experience is integrated into the classroom" (Delli Carpini & Keeter, 2000, p. 636). This is a "best practices" and evaluation criterion: A project must provide substantive description of the program and how service-learning was defined and implemented.

Studies on volunteering and on service-learning have similar findings. A study of young people's experiences of volunteering showed that this accurately predicts their choosing similar activities as adults (Andolina, Jenkins, Zukin, & Keeter, 2003). In contrast, Cone (2003) found that when volunteer or service activities are not properly guided, students may have prejudicial and discriminatory attitudes reinforced, not challenged or ameliorated. This is seen as antithetical to positive citizen engagement. He also suggested that students might come to see themselves as benefactors to these communities in the old model of "friendly visitor" and the benevolent outsider. Many would argue that this view does not capture the meanings of democratic citizenship (Boyte, 1991; Boyte & Farr, 1997). These findings also suggest that service as an approach to civic engagement might mislead those who want their exposure to service to enhance the likelihood of their current and lifelong citizen engagement. Clearly, embedded in all of this is a moral reading of the citizen role, of a civic involvement ideology as such, and of particular philosophies, beliefs, and values. None of this can be avoided, for *service, volunteer, participation, engagement, community,* and *democracy* are all political terms. So, too, is *community change.*

Social/community change

"Young people are a force for social change and innovation" (Africa News Service, 2003). This phrase captures the ethos of this third approach to youth civic engagement. In this approach, the primary concern is how to involve young people in community and/or social change initiatives. This approach was designed after service-learning practitioners questioned its effectiveness (e.g., Boyte, 1991). Proponents of this strategy argue that the best way to educate young people for citizenship is for them to be engaged in actual and real community and social change (Rogers, Mediratta, & Shah, 2012). In this approach, young people are invited to participate directly in improving their own communities, or in working with a social advocacy group (e.g., Cammarota & Fine, 2008; Delgado & Staples, 2008). Young people can contribute to their communities even at a young age, proponents argue (Checkoway & Richards-Schuster, 2003; Finn & Checkoway, 1998). Support for this approach is found within public work theory (Boyte, 1991), the philosophy of Paulo Freire (1970), action research (Cammarota & Fine, 2008), and evaluation studies (Driskell, 2002; McNiff, 2002; Sabo Flores, 2008; Stringer, 1996). This approach supports young people in identifying issues of public concern that matter to them, working together with others to devise and implement strategies, then evaluating these strategies to determine what work remains to be done (Boyte & Skelton, 1997; Chawla, 2002; Hart, 1999). Most often emphasized in this approach is the idea of participation, meaning that all decisions that affect young people are made together with young people (Hart, 1992). As such, this approach often has an improvisational, jazz-like feel to it. Decisions regarding what to do; how to do it; and who will do what, when, and how, are all decided by the entire group, regardless of member age or group size (Boyte & Skelton, 1997). That young people have an opportunity to choose what to do, and how, distinguishes this approach. But making these activities available and accessible to young people has been of primary concern. Seen in this third broad approach are the constructivist assumptions about the young person and the sociopolitical philosophy and ideology of youth participation and engagement. There are examples of this approach in action.

The 1960s Freedom Schools are an example. Their purpose was "to enable students to articulate the desire for change that was awakened by the questions they were being empowered to ask," and then to jointly act with others on these "desires" (Chilcoat & Ligon, 2001, p. 214). Here, youth voice is joined to participation, and both are linked to citizen. These schools supported students in three ways: by increasing their awareness of the issues that were affecting, experienced as affecting, and seen to affect their lives; by providing them with guidance as to how to act on this awareness; and by inviting them to evaluate their actions

(Chilcoat & Ligon, 2001). Freedom Schools started by critically examining the lives of the participants using a critical inquiry based on dialogue among all present. This proved to encourage young people to express themselves, and to participate in multiple roles (participant, facilitator, researcher, etc.), develop group loyalty, and clarify their individual strengths and weaknesses. This process was linked to highlighted inequalities and injustices within communities, and invited young people to work on reformist responses. In one case, the group worked together to enroll Black children in a formerly all-White elementary school (Chilcoat & Ligon, 1998). After each work stage, the group evaluated their own and others' work. This cycle of address & response to group development, to action, to evaluation, to improvement is basic to our conception of a civic youth worker.

This approach has recently received much attention. Both new theoretical conceptions of youth development (Ginwright, Cammarota, & Noguera, 2005), and the publication of many studies (Cammarota & Fine, 2008; Ginwright, 2010; Ginwright, Noguera, & Cammarota, 2006), have been used to name and integrate principles and practices into youth programs. An early study by Zeldin, McDaniel, Topitzes, and Calvert (2000), found that involving young people in the work of the governing boards of community organizations led adults to change their perceptions of young people, increasing both adults' and young people's commitment to the organization. In another study, Rafferty (2001) noticed that young people were no longer defined by their age after most took on adult responsibilities and acted in "grown-up ways" (p. 9). Most of the other findings on this approach do not come from formal studies, but rather from the "practice wisdom" of longtime workers. Driskell (2002) argued that having young people participate in community development has multiple benefits to young people, to other members of the community, and to policy-makers and urban planners. Others have commented on how this approach opens up spaces where young people can be "social change agents," and this often results in young people having greater "ownership" of the work (Driskell, 2002; Finn & Checkoway, 1998; Rafferty, 2001). This third approach emphasizes changes in the world and in the self. The last approach focuses on the latter, the young person.

Individual development

The fourth and final approach recognizes youth civic engagement as an individual developmental process (Gibson, 2001). This does not happen overnight or through learning specific skills or knowledge. Rather, it depends on young people forming a civic identity over time (Youniss, McLellan, & Yates, 1997). Within this developmental understanding, civic engagement is located within the larger psychosocial development of a young person. In this approach, civic engagement depends on young people "developing" "a strong sense of personal identity, responsibility, caring, compassion and tolerance prior to being engaged politically or at the community level" (Gibson, 2001). Young people cannot be expected to develop a strong civic identity if they do not receive basic support for their own development. Programs that support "healthy youth development" can also be seen to support youth civic engagement, because youth see "that actions are interdependent, that group discipline serves a common purpose, that differences among participants can be negotiated, and that multiple perspectives can be coordinated" (Youniss, McLellan, & Yates, 1997, p. 624). This approach serves to illustrate how classical and innovative youth development programs can also be places for youth civic engagement, and thus for the development of a citizen and/or civic identity.

Any effort to support young people's healthy development, such as those which are programmatic in YMCAs, YWCAs, the Boy Scouts, Camp Fire girls, the Girl Scouts, and 4-H, could qualify on these terms. Such efforts are given particular attention in this approach because these often provide both practice in participating and supportive ideological orientations. Young people experience "normative civic practices," including working together with others and taking responsibility for their actions; they are also exposed to particular worldviews (Youniss, McLellan, & Yates, 1997, p. 630). The Boy Scouts is a clear example. Scout troops are effective when young people jointly decide and together complete tasks. A troop can be an opportunity to practice several forms of leadership by taking on different leadership positions available, i.e., Senior Patrol Leader, Patrol Leader, etc. Young people are exposed to a particular worldview through the Boy Scout oath, law, motto, and slogan, as illustrated by their oath:

> On my honor I will do my best; To do my duty to God and my country and to obey the Scout Law; To help other people at all times; To keep myself physically strong, mentally awake, and morally straight.

Youth development programs are widespread, all with the purpose of supporting young people's psychosocial development, yet varying greatly in philosophy, goals, approaches, and substance. Civic engagement is grafted onto this tree. For decades, these classic organizations took for granted their positive contribution to the development of young people. In recent years, research and evaluation have supported this conclusion of programmatic effectiveness.

Evidence supporting youth development efforts as a way to enhance youth civic engagements short to long term, come from research on politically active adults, i.e., retrospective studies. These found that young people who participated in high school extracurricular activities were more likely as adults to vote and join community organizations (Youniss, McLellan, & Yates, 1997). Participation in extracurricular activities has also been linked to healthy youth development in the forms of reduced high-school dropouts and lower criminal activity (Eccles, Barber, Stone, & Hunt, 2003), supporting the first step toward youth civic engagement as proposed by this approach. Obviously, this is parallel to issues in the study of health and illness: Is the absence of illness "health?" Or is "health" a different, positive status, as the World Health Organization (WHO) promotes?

That is, is healthy youth development the absence or lower rates of school dropouts, or is it better conceived of differently, in positive terms? Here, too, is the finding that in the US at least, it is easier to study the specifics of a negative condition than a positive one because the American (English) language is more specific to the negative than to the positive, as in illness compared to health. This, in part, may be an outcome of the work of "moral statisticians" who studied suicide, criminality, and other "moral conditions" such as poverty. In a book on civic youth work, the "political arithmeticians," too, deserve a footnote, for their practice of gauging the power and strength of a ruler by the size of his military, i.e., number of horses, men in armor, and the rest. Remember that these terms and, as will be shown, civic youth work in its essentials, are political-moral, with civic youth work a moral enterprise in the civic realm.

These activities also have been shown to be contexts in which adolescents can be active producers of their own development (Dworkin, Larson, & Hansen, 2003), further supporting youth agency and the influence of this on individual development. Yet, other research has found weak some of these research-based claims.

Zaff, Malanchuk, Michelsen, & Eccles (2003), found evidence to support "the perspective that integrating civic education with civic experiences will result in higher percentages of youth becoming involved in civic activities," although this alone often did not predict adult civic participation (p. 21). Also necessary are young people's social support, socioeconomic status, and culture. Another study also found that youth civic engagement depends on the presence of several factors, and that the simple correlation of co-curricular school activities and youth civic engagement and lifelong involvement are not causative and not easy to "boost in a single stroke" (Andolina, Jenkins, Zukin, & Keeter, 2003). This research suggests that there is more to it than one condition, belief, or action. It is by now true that co-curricular school activities are important for producing youth civic engagement, but this alone will not predict future, adult civic participation. Since this last theme fits for each type of youth civic engagement, we are left with the question:

What can be said with certainty about what brings about youth's lifelong civic engagement? This we engage next.

Analyzing Youth Civic Engagement

While each of the approaches promotes a particular image and understanding of citizenship, all agree that one exists, but there is yet no agreement on what it is: metaphysics! Not having agreed-upon conceptions or definitions is troubling to those who believe that this hinders scholarship on youth civic engagement (Sherrod, Flanagan, & Youniss, 2002). They argue that without a definition, researchers cannot learn which factors are most important or predictive to adult civic participation, and hence they cannot evaluate current strategies and practices. Without definitional clarity, they argue, empirical research cannot be done: this is classic Positivism. It ignores the fifty years of scholarship on definitions, meanings, epistemology, and alternate research paradigms and methods (e.g., Cohen, Kahn, & Steeves, 2000; Gadamer, 1985; van Manen, 1990), and especially important here, youth voice, youth meanings and conceptions, youth experiences, youth opinions, and youth truths.

Too often scholars categorize projects on the program name, formal ethos, and presented program descriptions—all adult sources. Missing are youth sources. Missing, too, is the actual style of work and approach of the program. The printed and the actual are different realities (VeLure Roholt, Hildreth, & Baizerman, 2008). To put similar-seeming programs in a category is, of course, to risk homogenizing differences in style, substance, talent, and the rest. Different actual programs may be phenotypically similar, but show real and different genotypic differences. This is partly a consequence of vocabulary and its use in this emergent field of practice and study, where basic conceptions, meanings-in-use, and definitions are still somewhat fluid, as shown. Internationally, the range and depth of diversity within the four categories of approaches to youth civic engagement are even greater. A viable alternative is to organize these categories by their image and understanding of young people and youth citizenship rather than by using program type.

This review of the basic concepts—*young people, citizen,* and *youth civic engagement*—discloses no strong agreement on many topics, including the most basic—youth civic engagement as program and as curriculum. Within the topics of civics, service, social change, and youth development, there are rich and diverse forms of practice, and these may have more in common with each other than with the category itself. To find family resemblances between and among programs, we should look at how they understand and implement in their work the basic notions of youth civic engagement, and hence, civic youth work: Civic youth work can be an overlay on all four approaches. We address this next.

Conclusions

This long and complex chapter presented the basic concepts of civic youth work, finding these in youth, citizen, civics, service, social change, and youth development. Shown was the home of each in recent scholarship, and the links purported between and among these and youth civic engagement, the short-term, processual goal of civic youth work; the longer, broader telos are lifelong civic literacy; civic engagement; and active, responsive, and responsible citizenship—citizen (public) work, volunteer or paid, part- or full-time, and (always) jointly with others on issues of meaning, importance, and consequence.

It was shown, often in passing, that each of these terms has politico-moral meanings in policy and practice, and that scholarship did not always study these, seeing instead scientific developmental "outcomes." Embedded in the reviewed images, rhetorics, models, theories, and concepts was the politico-moral. This matters, because civic youth work as a field, as programs/projects/initiatives, and as practice is a politico-moral enterprise. That this is so does not diminish the potential utility of scientific, social, and developmental research within any epistemological frame, but such scholarship will be put to practical teloi—human development of young people as lifelong citizens, human citizen(ship)-making, if you will.

From these academic concerns, we now move closer to the ground of everyday life, with an exploration in three chapters of our conceptions of civic youth work.

Reflective Questions

1. How do you in your everyday, scholarly, and professional modes and worlds distinguish between and among: adolescent, young person, youth, youthhood, teenager, young people?
2. What are the everyday, scholarly, and professional biographies of the basic concepts and/or terms designating youth where you live?
3. How does chronological age work as a sociolegal and sociopolitical criterion?

Glossary

Biophysiological development: From this perspective, our cognitive, social, and behavioral development is joined to our body's physical maturation. It asserts that the maturity stages of our bodies are accurate predictors of capacity and capability.

Civic literacy: The skills and knowledge to act effectively as a member of a community.

Contested Concept: Describes particular concepts that do not have an agreed, fixed definition.

Image of the young person: How media, society, and often scholarship conceptualizes, imagines, and represents the age category of young people. These images are based on stereotypical and discriminatory understandings of young people, and while they connect to young people's everyday, lived experience, they are misleading, reductionist, and misinforming about who young people really are.

Recapitulation process: Proposed by G. Stanley Hall (1904), this theory posited that young people follow a similar developmental pathway to societies, moving from savage to civilized as one ages. This theoretical model helped to foster the image of adolescence as a period of "storm and stress." Although disproven in multiple, rigorous, academic and scholarly studies around the world, the image of adolescence as time of crisis and turmoil remains.

Youth: In everyday usage youth refers to the time of life when one is young. In the field of youth studies, this concept is used to designate how young people come to be conceptualized at different historical moments and within different cultures. Often disclosed by the question: What does it mean, to whom, to be and to do a certain age, around here now?

Youthhood: The cultural and historical patterns of growing up. The ways society(ies) have organized the everyday experience for people who are recognized as not children anymore, but not yet adults.

3

Civic Youth Work:
The Program

Civic youth work is composed of two constituents: a civic youth work initiative/project/program, and civic youth work(er) practice. We begin with the program(matic). Remember that a goal of a civic youth work program is to move away from the status of project or initiative or program to become "the ways that things typically are done around here," i.e., sociopolitical and cultural change which makes ordinary and visible this form of youth work with young people.

We begin with three short case studies, or better, program narratives. Each is then read from three perspectives—what does this narrative disclose and teach about how this project specifically sees youth/young person/young people? Second, what does this narrative disclose and teach about how this specific project sees youth citizen(ship) and lived citizen(ship)? Third, what does this narrative disclose and teach about how this specific project sees civic youth work(er) practice? These three project narratives and the three readings of each become data which are read again to pick out themes around the three nodes: youth, citizen, and youth work. The case studies introduce some central ideas and concepts which are the base of civic youth work. This chapter is followed by two chapters which take on, explore, and analyze civic youth work practice and being a civic youth worker.

We take this idea from a book on reading zoos, by Malamud (1998), where he distinguished five reading stances:

- Reading about zoos,
- Reading through zoos (to challenge them),
- Reading against zoos,
- Reading beyond zoos, and
- Reading zoos themselves.

Adapting his structural, positional idea, one can read about youth civic engagement and civic youth work to learn about these, and one could read these to get at notions of youth embodied in, laced through, or absent from civic youth work and youth civic engagement. Similarly, one could begin with young people and read civic youth work and youth civic engagement from that perspective. There are other obvious permutations of this. One value in reading this way is to get at the explicit and implicit relations between and among the ideas, from contingency to inextricability—from a sometime relation to one which cannot easily be unwound or separated. Much of the literature, when read this way, is asymmetric, with writings on youth citizenship not obliged to mention youth activism, and their participation, involvement, and engagement, while read in the other direction, youth rarely disappears from writings on youth civic engagement and civic youth work. We use this idea to read each of the case studies.

To introduce civic youth work, we use three case studies of civic youth work in three regions of the world. The first is historical, and describes the work of the Mississippi Freedom School in the United States during the 1950s and 1960s Civil Rights Movement. The second is from Northern Ireland and Ireland and describes the work of Youth Bank from the 1990s until today. Finally, a description of a recent initiative in India, PUKAR, is presented. While each has its own particular focus, they are programmatically similar, in that all seek to invite and support young people to work on civic and political issues that are meaningful and consequential to themselves (and possibly others).

Freedom Schools

The Freedom Schools are a good historical example of Civic Youth Work. They were founded by the Student Nonviolent Coordinating Committee (SNCC). Founded in 1960, SNCC played a major role in the U.S. Civil Rights Movement. This organization was staffed by mostly young, Black leaders (most members were between 15–22 years old), and "chose to concentrate [on] injustice in the rural counties of the Deep South" (Stoper, 1977, p.18). They first worked to integrate public spaces (lunch counters, bus stations) throughout the South, and with this mostly accomplished, they moved on to voter registration (Stoper, 1977). Freedom Schools became one of SNCC's efforts to address U.S. racial injustice. Their purpose, as stated by its organizers, was "to help [students] begin to question" (Chilcoat & Ligon, 2001). Freedom Schools sought to provide an alternative public school by inviting young people to think about issues that mattered most to them and their everyday, lived experience.

The school was six to eight weeks long. School facilitators and teachers received SNCC training (Chilcoat & Ligon, 1998b). Rather than encouraging a specific instruction methodology, the schools emphasized student democratic participation. While Freedom Schools focused on teaching students how sociopolitical and historical forces shaped their lives, they emphasized discussion, questioning, and action over more didactic methods. Discussion as such was seen as an empowering of students to solve real problems (Chilcoat & Ligon, 2001). Instructors sought to invite young people to take an active role in their own lives and education. The curriculum was based on democratic principles and focused on social justice.

The curriculum was built on the experiences students brought to class; instructors focused discussion on these, raising questions to learn more about them, and then with students planning and taking thoughtful action on these (Chilcoat & Ligon, 1998b). It sought to provide experiences that facilitated young people in becoming conscious of the sociopolitical, historical, political, and economic forces shaping their lives, how to challenge authority (especially White authority), and learn to think on their own and take action (Chilcoat & Ligon, 1998b). A major curriculum focus was learning to formulate and ask questions.

Asking questions was seen as a first step in how young people could move from passive to active engagement with their learning and the larger world (Chilcoat & Ligon, 1998b). Using discussion, young people were invited to think critically about their experiences and beliefs. This work was done democratically, teaching this, too, experientially. For example, discussions followed a three-step process:

1. Introductory questions asking students about their feelings on an idea or experience,
2. Questions getting at why they feel the way they do, and
3. How do we (instructors and youth) feel about each other's reactions to these ideas (Chilcoat & Ligon, 2001, p. 215).

Also important as a byproduct of the discussions was teaching students important "soft" skills, including: taking part in discussions about issues of importance to them, how to listen to others, how to facilitate discussions, and how to move a discussion toward decision and community action (Chilcoat & Ligon, 1998b). Discussions in Freedom Schools often were focused around a problem or issue, and always involved soliciting students' views, clarifications, criticisms, and analysis. This was participatory learning.

While a primary focus was asking students to bring issues to the class, Freedom Schools also used case studies of societal issues, a citizenship curriculum, and a text called, *The Guide to Negro History* (Chilcoat & Ligon, 1998b). Case studies were used to introduce ideas, and the young people/students were encouraged to look at how a case study touched their personal experiences and the sociocultural and political situation in Mississippi. They were asked also to consider possible responses to these community and sociocultural problems. The citizenship curriculum asked students to identify what from their own lives, such as the challenges they faced, might they now understand as connected to the broader, oppressive society in which they lived, and how their experience in the Freedom Schools differed (Chilcoat & Ligon, 1998b). The citizenship curriculum challenged young people to examine their lives critically, and to consider how to take action to create social change. Activities often focused on sociopolitical history and culture, current events, voter registration, and community organizing (Chilcoat & Ligon, 1998b). Freedom Schools used a variety of methods, including theater, to solicit young people's lived experiences and to invite their comments.

Developing group dramas further supported building discussion skills and other soft skills. The hope was that students would be able to translate experiences from the plays into real-life problem-solving and social action. This is an early example of "theater of the oppressed" (Boal, 1979). Building theater followed a similar process as group discussions:

> beginning with a problem or problems to be solved; becoming aware of the problem and the need for a solution; analyzing the problem according to students' experiences, knowledge, attitudes and practices; gathering and interpreting information; considering a number of viewpoints; comparing a variety of possible solutions; formulating and testing possibilities; clarifying and defining the problem and its solution by organizing the information into a concrete story; turning the story into a series of dramatic situations; performing the play in such a way that it provides a solution to the problem (Chilcoat & Ligon,1998a, p. 537).

Plays were always debriefed in a process similar to the one used in the three-step discussion process (described above). Theater was seen also to develop a sense of group responsibility, and a space for group members to share and reflect on their individual strengths and weaknesses (Chilcoat & Ligon, 1998a). A final focus of the Freedom Schools was on developing students' academic skills in reading, writing, and speaking. Curriculum was always built from student experiences and used a discussion method, but also emphasized building academic skills (Emery et al., 2004). All theater and other learning activities had to support a common ethos.

The ethos of the Freedom Schools was "social responsibility, grassroots democracy, and critical citizenship" (Chilcoat & Ligon, 1998b, p. 168). This was fostered by the learning environment and by learning practices. In the schools' view, young people were both learners and potential social-change agents. They were taught to question and challenge, and to take specific action in the world. The young people were learners and teachers—learning from their own engagement in group discussions, and contributing to the learning of their age-mates (Chilcoat & Ligon, 1998b). In contrast to the Mississippi public schools, where learning meant "learning to stay in your place" (Chilcoat & Ligon, 1998b, p. 171), the Freedom Schools provided a rich education in typical and unique subjects and methods, using a participatory pedagogy.

Reading Freedom Schools through youth

Freedom Schools had an atypical, even radical understanding of young people—as critical thinkers and workers for social change. This conception challenged both the racist and **ageist** understandings of young Blacks at this historical moment, and continues to serve as an example to counter still prevalent deficit images of young people (Belton, 2009; Males, 1996). Freedom Schools sought to challenge the **disenfranchisement** and second-class status of young people promoted by official racist and ageist policy, a situation that continues (Ginwright, Cammarota, & Noguera, 2005). Freedom Schools' staff would agree that "youth have the right to participate in policies that affect them" (Ginwright, Cammarota, & Noguera, 2005, p. 33). Given this, the Freedom School curriculum was based on perceiving and acting toward the students in a manner that perceived young people as able to critically analyze their everyday lived and larger reality, and sought to use this to guide their collective social action.

Reading Freedom Schools through citizen(ship)

Freedom Schools did not advocate a normative understanding of citizen(ship)—
wherein one presumed equal rights and equal opportunity under the law; and these
included voting and belonging to a political party. Freedom Schools did not see the
country and its policies as benevolent (Banks, 1997; Ginwright & Cammarota,
2002). This rightfully influenced its definition of citizen. Freedom Schools provided a critical citizenship education to counter the normative definition, which
often instructed young, Black people to follow directions and do as told. They
would clearly agree with contemporary scholarship on citizenship education that
argues:

> *Citizenship education* has been constructed historically by powerful and main-
> stream groups and has usually served their interest. It has often fostered citizen
> passivity rather than action, taught students large doses of historical myths in its
> attempts to develop patriotism, conceptualized citizenship responsibility primar-
> ily as voting, and reinforced the dominant social, racial, and class inequity in
> American society. In other words, citizenship education in the United States has
> historically reinforced dominant-group hegemony and student inaction (Banks,
> 1997, p. 4).

Freedom Schools saw young people as contributors today; creators of a more
inclusive, socially just, and nonviolent present and future society. They supported
active youth citizenship: citizens as engaged on real, meaningful, and consequential topics, issues, problems, or concerns. They invited and supported an activism
directed at an ongoing public challenge to public policies and practices that were
racist, unjust, and unfair. The job of the citizens was to work to create a better society for all citizens.

Reading Freedom Schools through civic youth work

Freedom Schools worked to engage young people in analysis and understanding
of contemporary issues, and to invite their participation in their own liberation—
as free persons living their freedom. They sought to build what we now call "**community social capital**": communities where "residents maintain intergenerational
ties, share information and advice with young people, and establish clear pathways
for civic participation for young people in community settings" (Ginwright,
Cammarota, & Noguera, 2005). Freedom Schools are a clear and early example of
youth/adult partnerships (Camino, 2000). Emphasis then was working with

young people, not only teaching to them, and on seeing these youth as both learners and teachers. This is a sentiment well understood in critical education theory and practice (Freire, 1970). It is clear that critical pedagogy is one base for civic youth work.

As seen in the case study, Freedom Schools focused on raising young people's awareness of the connection between and among social relationships, public policy, and their everyday lived experiences. But the work did not end with young people developing a more critical understanding of their situation; they were also invited and supported to act on this new information. Staff (civic youth workers) supported students both to learn about their situation and also to explore how they might act on issues they found meaningful and important so as to improve their everyday lived experiences—supporting both reflection and action (Freire, 1970). This model has supported several participatory approaches to working with young people.

Freedom Schools then, maybe more than in their contemporary form, were civic youth work sites—in conception, ethos, structure, and practice. Sixty years old, they still fit current realities, and are still needed in the US and internationally. Then and now, freedom is more an idea than lived. This is true for many, especially so for youth. When life does not teach freedom and how it is lived, produced, protected, and sustained, this must be learned somewhere—even in a school. The next case study of Youth Bank provides a contemporary program model based in youth participation.

Youth Bank

Youth Bank (YB) is a youth philanthropic initiative. It supports the creation and management of local youth grant-giving committees. It aims to address social needs in local communities, support active youth citizenship, support young people developing knowledge and skills in governance, and build young people's capacity around a range of skills. Based on the Council of Michigan Foundation's Youth Grant-making Initiative, Youth Bank in Northern Ireland and Ireland now supports sites throughout Ireland and Northern Ireland, as well as international sites in Armenia, Turkey, Serbia, and Azerbaijan.

Youth Bank's strategy is youth-led grant-making and grant-monitoring. It supports young people learning in small groups about important issues in their communities and then provides funding to community organizations and young people to address these. To support group activity and work, YB supports both capacity-building in research, grant-making, monitoring, and evaluation. It also provides ongoing personal development for individual group members, including certification in grant-giving, as well as training in interview skills, democratic decision-making, grant application scoring, funding decision-making, and fundraising. The organization is strongly committed to group work and youth participation.

All YB committees are expected to work together to get the job done. The strategy includes a focus on building a strong group in order to strengthen the quality of the work. Committee members participate in group-building exercises, discuss controversial issues, and engage in team challenges to learn how they could better work together within YB. Having an effective group is important because the group controls how the work gets done. As one participant said: "structure is not set in stone, groups are allowed to put own spin on it." With this flexibility and the option to choose different methods and means for the work, committee members have to figure out how to accomplish what they were asked to do.

Youth Bank supports a range of grant-giving activities, including: research, forming criteria, advertising, receiving applications, assessing and scoring applications, interviewing applicants, making final decisions about grant-giving, presentation of awardees, monitoring and evaluation, and finally, celebration. Like many youth civic engagement initiatives, Youth Bank is organized as a group activity. Participants are chosen through a variety of methods, some more selective than others, with initial activity focused on group and team building. The first activity the group focuses on, especially if it is newly formed, is research. At this stage, the group wants to learn the range of issues young people are facing in their community. Participants analyze the research and negotiate as a group what the data teach about local community needs and wants. What they decide is used to develop their criteria for funding priorities. Funding applications are then targeted toward these needs. Once the criteria have been established, the group advertises and creates public awareness of the grant money, and encourages groups of young people to apply. While much of the work up until this point is small-group focused, beginning in the next stage more young people are included.

Rather than simply advertise and wait for applications, Youth Bank groups generally are more proactive and meet with prospective groups, assisting them in writing their applications and providing feedback and training on how to write a good application. Once applications have been received, each is read and assessed using the group-created criteria. Assessing the applications is also supported with internal YB training. Here, young people discuss with a facilitator why the process must be fair and transparent, and how they can implement these principles. They also interview all those who submit applications. These interviews are used to gauge whether the idea truly came from young people, and whether their inclusion in the grant is merely tokenistic. Also during the interview, the panel probes for more information, and asks for clarification. The groups realize that writing an application for funding is a difficult task, one that young people do not have much experience doing. Therefore, the interview process is used as an informal education space where applicants receive technical consultation from the YB team, and the YB team collects necessary additional information for the committee to make its informed and reflective decisions. After all of the interviews, the group collectively discusses all the applicants and selects those to receive funding.

The announcement of who received funding is a time for celebration. Youth Bank groups want to acknowledge young people's work securing this funding. From this point until the next funding cycle, YB committees work with funded programs to ensure implementation fidelity and accountability. They monitor and evaluate how money is being used and whether it fits the group's proposal. The grant-making cycle ends with a celebration of achievement. This stage aims to highlight the accomplishments of the grant cycle and celebrate the hard work of the community groups and the YB team.

Throughout the entire process two major values are emphasized: shared understanding and shared decision-making—and these contribute to the overall YB ethos. These succinctly describe YB's model of youth participation. In places where young people are often treated as not having the ability to participate, YB commitment to shared decision-making and understanding creates a democratic space for learning and community action. This work also begins to describe a different kind of relationship between adults and young people: adults as allies. Young people remain central to the decision-making process with the assistance and support of adults. The adults help young people to do what they want at a higher level. They scaffold (Rogoff, 1990) the experience, so that young people can gain a mastery over process and content that otherwise is unavailable.

Reading Youth Bank through youth

Youth Bank like the Freedom School challenges typical, normative ways of understanding young people by emphasizing young people as competent (Lansdown, 2005) and capable (Biggeri, Ballet, & Comim, 2011) (or able to quickly become competent and capable) decision-makers, and by extension, competent community builders (Finn & Checkoway, 1998). With its emphasis on youth voice and participation, the case study illuminates how young people are understood in the context of the **United Nations Convention on the Rights of the Child** (UNCRC).

Acknowledging and agreeing with ongoing and insightful criticism of the UNCRC, especially issues around the lack of cultural considerations with its age-based definitions of *young person* and *child* (Skelton, 2008), this document still contains a bold and contemporary vision for understanding and providing support for young people internationally. It emphasizes three conceptual frameworks: provision, protection, and participation. Each of these receives attention in YB.

Most obvious is participation, with YB's emphasis on youth voice and young people's involvement in naming what issues are important for them (in their communities). This understanding of young people also supports YB's overall focus on shared understanding and shared decision-making, allowing young people to take responsibility for major funding decisions. The case study also emphasizes the other two foci, although less straightforwardly. Through assessing community needs and then providing funding to support programs and initiatives to address these, YB directly implements the idea of provision. It seeks to enhance the overall level of youth service in an area directed at enhancing youth wellness, health, and development. Finally, YB also provides protection to young people, both through programmatic structure and programs supported. Young people on funding committees have greater protection in their community, because they work with each other and also because of organization and staff support. Structures such as YB have been found to be both participatory and protective (Child Protection Working Group, 2012; Rizvi, 2012). All of these provide young people protection, and also ensure that youth voice and youth perspective is noticed and heard by the larger community.

Reading Youth Bank through citizen(ship)

Citizen(ship) receives a slightly different definition in YB than in the Freedom Schools. While in many ways more normative, their conception is inclusive, active, and creative citizenship (Weller, 2007). Program structure and the grant cycle support greater youth understanding and addressing of community problems. YB also raises awareness of issues young people may be facing that are unnoticed or unnamed, such as exclusion from certain public spaces, discriminatory treatment by certain community members or groups, or simply the lack of any public opportunities for youth recreation and informal learning. YB participants are involved in what in the US is called "public work" (Boyte & Farr, 1997). Through their committee participation, young people create new and innovative ways of addressing community issues, both through targeting funding priorities and also through supporting other young people to respond to these issues. Weller's (2007) description of youth citizenship initiatives could easily be used to describe Youth Bank as well: "Through their own creativity, innovation and social networks, [young people] have succeeded in changing and improving their local environments, thus challenging the notion of teenage apathy. They have established themselves as committed political actors" (p. 168).

How Youth Bank understands young people and citizenship together supports participatory practice with young people—another basis for civic youth work. Youth Bank shows that a heretofore adult prerogative, one thought to require, if not demand, adult control and participation, is shown to be grounded, enriched, and well-executed by young people. It is all in the expectations held for the youth, their training, and continued adult support—civic youth work in action.

Reading Youth Bank through civic youth work

Youth Bank is a model for participatory work with youth, another way of understanding civic youth work. A basic framework for understanding this practice comes from Hart (1992) and his ladder of participation (Chapter Two). This eight-rung ladder describes how practice can be understood as either nonparticipatory (manipulation, decoration, or tokenism) or participatory (assigned but informed; consulted and informed; adult-initiated, shared decisions with children; child-initiated and directed; and child-initiated, shared decisions with adults) (Hart, 1992). While much of current scholarship on youth participation often starts with this model, the practice has been advocated by scholars and practitioners for decades.

Participatory youth work approaches like Youth Bank create real and meaningful roles for young people, and support their participation. While the Convention on the Rights of the Child does codify young people's right to participate, and has supported in many countries structures and opportunities for young people to give opinions on matters that affect them, these efforts have rarely produced noticeable changes in policy or program (Percy-Smith, 2010). Percy-Smith (2010) argued that this is often because youth participation remains focused on consultation, rather than on creating an "active process of involvement in learning and change" (p. 110). YB provides a model of how young people's involvement in learning and change can be supported and deepened.

This model includes what many youth programs tend to focus on exclusively, ongoing and quite extensive training and personal development opportunities. Unlike other youth programs, these activities are not ends in themselves, but rather are necessary so that young people can more actively and skillfully do real and meaningful work for other young people and for their community. Trainings support young people to do the group's work. Remarkably, Youth Bank appears to avoid the problems that have arisen with other youth participatory initiatives, which often focus exclusively on either consulting with young people, or preparing them for action, and young people never seem to be able to put what they have said or learned into action. Youth Bank's strategy teaches how to create rich and meaningful youth participatory structures, strategies, and actions. Young people also learn to do participatory action research and program evaluation. This is the primary strategy used by PUKAR, the last case example.

PUKAR Youth Fellowship Program

Partners in Urban Knowledge, Action and Research (PUKAR) is a nongovernmental organization in Mumbai, India. It aims to democriatize how research is done. It believes that nonexpert—indigenous (Chilisa, 2012) and citizen—knowledge can contribute to problem-solving, on the local to international levels. While PUKAR operates different programs, the Urban Youth and Knowledge Production research theme, and its Youth Fellowship Program (YFP), are the foci of this narrative.

The multiple aims of YFP focus around two primary agendas:

1. To provide opportunities for young people to see themselves as researchers and community organizers for social change, and
2. To build their capacities to do these effectively (http://pukar.org.in/yf/).

Building from Arjun Appadurai's (2006) essay, "The Right to Research," YFP believes that young people are capable of doing meaningful research on their own lives, and on community and society topics, and of taking action using that research on issues of importance to them to create social change on local, regional, national, and global levels.

YFP works to develop the capacity of its participants to "access the right information from the right source, process it, evaluate it and then make an informed decision about their life and career opportunities as well as the political systems which shape and sway them deeply" (http://pukar.org.in/yf/about/principle/). The traditional Indian education system, focused on the memorization of established facts and expert knowledge, is seen as failing to engage students in this important work. YFP's other aim involves the participants' developing necessary "soft skills," including: motivation, ability to meet challenges, accountability, tolerance, and conflict management. These are seen as also neglected in traditional education. YFP sees young people as researchers and uses experiential and critical pedagogies to support their ongoing development as active, competent, and ethical researchers on real-world topics.

YFP's strategy is to engage young people to take active roles in their learning, in becoming researchers, and in becoming producers of knowledge. The YFP "uses research as a pedagogical, interventional, and advocacy tool to empower youth to negotiate the city and focuses on transforming the quality of life in Mumbai" (http://pukar.org.in/yf/about/). YFP does this by recognizing the learner's knowledge and using this as a base for learning. Part of the learner's knowledge is personal and is in part about their experiences of and in the city. YFP believes that these experiences and understandings are the base upon which individual participation on social transformation can be mobilized.

The YFP curriculum is based in critical pedagogical traditions (e.g., Freire, 1970), which challenge the "banking" concept of learning and emphasize instead engagement and active learning strategies (Duncan-Andrade & Morrell, 2008). In YFP, this manifests in the learner becoming the knowledge producer. The process of recognizing one's self as a researcher and then conducting research "transforms research into a pedagogical tool" (http://pukar.org.in/pukar-home/projects/project1/).

In YFP, young people choose topics from their neighborhoods and their everyday lives that they wish to learn about. Young people form into groups of ten to twelve and work with PUKAR staff for a full year to transform their topic into a completed research project. Of course, this process involves developing research questions, choosing methodologies, collecting and analyzing data, and report writing. Training in research methodologies and techniques includes "mapping, census taking, interviewing and archival methods" (http://pukar.org.in/yf/about/history/). The projects end with final results shared publically.

Young people in YFP participate in numerous activities, including: educational and experiential workshops on the research process and on topics related to their research questions, interregional collaboration between other youth on research projects, meetings with adult program coordinators, hosting and participating in community and regional events to share research, public speaking and outreach activities in a variety of contexts, organizing discussions, and the production of media resources. YFP involves traditional forms of learning (lectures, dialogues, and film screenings), action-learning (Argyris, 1993), and experiential learning (Boud, Cohen, & Walker, 1993).

The YFP ethos is grounded in democracy and participation. Young people are seen as experts in their own lives, localities, and neighborhoods, and thus are most capable of observing and documenting local situations meaningful for their research. Young people's roles include not only knowledge consumer but also knowledge producer and learner. Young people are encouraged to participate in creating social and political change. Young people become active, engaged citizens (http://pukar.org.in/pukar-home/projects/project1/).

Reading PUKAR through youth

When invited, trained, and supported, young people are knowledge-producers, who can speak back to their life conditions. **Youth participatory action research** (YPAR), PUKAR's method, increasingly has been used to engage young people "in multigenerational collectives for critical inquiry and action" (Cammarota & Fine, 2008, p. 4). They are coresearchers who explore their local community and critically reflect on their learning, with the understanding that they will take collective action to address emergent issues. They are seen as "self-determining," and "a distinct presence in the world, as people who have the ability to make informed and intentional choices to guide action (Reason, 1994, p. 41). Young people are seen as both dependent and increasingly interdependent on others, and autonomous (Christian, 2003); as individuals with their own understandings, talents, and knowledge to be contributed. This challenges local and the almost universal views of young people as controlled by biology, and as not yet ready to participate fully in (adult) civic affairs.

Reading PUKAR through citizen(ship)

PUKAR is an active, emancipatory, critical, and collaborative understanding of youth citizenship. In the context of youth participatory evaluation, Kim Sabo Flores (2008) described this understanding of young people and of youth citizenship:

> Through participatory evaluation and research projects, young people often have opportunities to become civically involved. This type of engagement often differs from more traditional "civic engagement" and "civic leadership" projects in that young people are immediately involved as full citizens—collecting data, advocating, rallying, organizing peers, holding public hearings, meeting officials, and conducting press conferences (pp. 14–15).

PUKAR understands citizenship as an accomplishment, something achieved through intentional action in contrast to a definition based on chronological age.

Theirs is a participatory definition. Citizens are those engaged in the work of democracy, community building, and political action (VeLure Roholt, Hildreth, & Baizerman, 2009), what is called here civic youth work.

Reading PUKAR through civic youth work

PUKAR is grounded in the idea: "documentation as intervention" (Appadurai, 2006, p. 175). Practice focuses on developing research capacity, a basic right to research (Appadurai, 2006). Like others worldwide (see Cammarota & Fine, 2008; and Park, Brydon-Miller, Hall, & Jackson, 1993), participatory action research is the frame and practice.

Participatory action research (PAR) is a collaborative research process, emphasizing "the political aspects of knowledge production" (Reason, 1994, p. 47). It is often described as a cyclical process, of action and reflection (Reason, 1994), which begins with a group exploring an issue or topic, which they learn more about and plan how to research. They do the research, collecting data and reflecting on the experience and the data, and develop action plans. PAR as a way of working with young people is called youth participatory action research (YPAR) (Cammarota & Fine, 2008); it is a civic youth work practice.

YPAR is focused on social justice and personal transformation. "YPAR is a formal resistance that leads to transformation—systematic and institutional change to promote social justice" (Cammarota & Fine, 2008, p. 2). As collaborative inquiry (civic) youth workers and young people investigate issues and policies and take action. This is civic youth work, with its emphasis on public issues and the engagement of young people both as learners and doers, as public actors in public realms and arenas, as citizens, not in the making, but as citizens now.

Reading across the Case Studies: Describing Civic Youth Work

What do these three case examples teach about what is civic youth work? First, that civic youth work, however named, is not a rare practice. It is being undertaken worldwide and written about by the initiatives and by scholars. Second, it has many names, typically programmatic titles such as Youth Bank, PUKAR, and Freedom Schools. Third, the practice is called variously, youth participatory action research, citizen development, youth civic engagement, citizenship, and public work, for example. Fourth, in writing the case studies, we did not name any of the projects, practices, skills, or knowledge as "civic youth work." That is our term, and is not (yet) widely used in scholarship or youth work talk, our work being the exception (VeLure Roholt, Baizerman, & Hildreth, 2013; VeLure Roholt, Hildreth, & Baizerman, 2008).

The narrative examples, written by us, were intended to show that there is ongoing work with youth which is neither seen as nor called "youth work" or "civic youth work." This means that it is the work as such, its ethos, craft orientation, practice, and skills which place it in the families of youth work and civic youth work: The question of "What are they trying to do and why?" gets one to the arena, the game, the players, and the play. These show the field of play we call civic youth work.

In its essentials, civic youth work is about a field, programs, projects, an initiative, practices, and skills. To what ends? To open and sustain places for young people to do and be citizens, whether called "public work(ers)," civic activists, engaged youth, or citizens; and to cocreate with young people spaces for the mastery, rehearsal, and performance of citizen in its several forms, using the many skills of group participation and group action. For us, the goal is not "healthy youth development," whether defined narrowly in adolescent development terms (Lerner & Steinberg, 2009), more broadly in programmatic terms (Delgado, 2002), or even politically, as, for example, "critical citizenship." The latter we divorce from development, and allow it to live independently in the political and social realms; we will accept critical citizen as a form of individual political development, however. The narrative examples teach about civic youth work field and civic youth work program.

Deepening and Enriching Civic Youth Work: The Field and Programs

Civic youth work is composed of a field of play and practice, programs, projects, and initiatives, supported by an ethos, a craft orientation, knowledge, and skills. The narratives will be read next to learn about the field and program. Our reading will disclose the core conceptual building blocks of the civic youth work field, where ideas, values, ideology, philosophy, and ethos come together.

Youth participation

Common to the three examples is **youth participation**—the most basic building block of civic youth work. Indeed, without youth participation there is no civic youth work; this is the bedrock, the most important philosophical touchstone of youth civic engagement. Youth participation can take many forms and shapes; youth voice is one (Percy-Smith & Thomas, 2010). In the examples, there were not spaces, processes, activities, or moments which in theory, if not in practice, excluded worker invitation, support, and the use of young people's contribution: this is the grounding and guiding ethos of the field of civic youth work. This holds whether or not youth participation is called "activism," "youth (civic) engagement," "youth resistance," "public work," or citizenship. How this young person is solicited, supported, and invited is civic youth work practice. Organized arrangements to encourage young people to participate are civic youth work programs, projects, and initiatives. The goal of the civic youth work field is to make and sustain youth participation as ongoing, mundane practices in all relevant spheres of everyday life and on all relevant levels and spaces, including school, neighborhood, community, city, and the like. Youth participation and youth voice become relevant differently in the context of citizenship.

Youth voice

Voice is one shape of youth participation. The three narrative examples of civic youth work have in common a laser-like attentiveness to and practice of an ongoing soliciting, supporting, and utilizing of the voice of participant youth—their right to literally and frequently speak themselves—joining spoken and written words to ideas. Whoever is the civic youth worker in the examples is the embodiment of this invitation to participate.

A major formalization of **youth voice** is as a human right, and thus a right of a child, youth, adolescent, teen, and young person. Foremost among formalized protocols enshrining this right is UNICEF's Convention on the Rights of the Child. Youth voice in the civic youth work context is to be used however they, as an action group, democratically choose, including: deciding on what issues address them and how they wish to respond to their issues, the governance of the group, and in the larger world, policy-making affecting them and others in the public sphere, research, and evaluation. Youth voice is common to the three examples.

Youth citizen(ship)

Youth participation and youth voice in the sociopolitical realm is citizen(ship)—youth doing and being citizen. *Citizen* is not a term used throughout the three examples, in their actual program materials, in their talk about their goals and work, or in their direct civic youth work practice. In a sense, it is an extra term, unneeded in the work except for sociopolitical purposes: to demonstrate that young people can do, and are able—i.e., have the "capacity" and "capability"—to do citizen work, and thus to challenge the belief that youth are not "ready" for citizenship. And to challenge, by extension, the very idea of "youth" as it is not used sociolegally (and by further extension, the notion that chronological age should continue as a proxy for "capacity," "capability," "readiness," and the like). Further challenged is the sociopolitical disenfranchisement of young people from the citizen sociolegal status, as codified in law and lived in theory and everyday social life and practice. Youth as an age group is not a minority population in many sociolegal jurisdictions, sociocultural places, and other lived spaces, yet youth are treated as such, excluded and marginalized because of their birth age and the sociocultural, legal, and other meanings attached to age.

The three narrative examples show the competency of young people properly invited and supported to be citizens: civic youth work practiced by a civic youth worker. These issues and realities are socioculturally, sociopolitically, socioeconomically, and sociolegally context-dependent.

Context, place, and time

The three examples show that all of this—how youth participation, youth voice, and **youth citizen** are lived and shaped—is context-dependent, place-specific, and time-bound. This is obvious, or should be. Different languages, different meanings, different sociopolitical, legal, and cultural systems, and all the rest, mean that the local matters deeply and profoundly in how all of this is given shape, noticed, spoken (about), understood, and practiced. Yet, there are (maybe) commonalities in the examples, if not universals.

These commonalities you know by now. More difficult is the question of our selection and reporting bias in presenting examples which make the finding of commonalities easy, and by so doing place the question of whether there are universals here at a horizon. We simply do not know. Yet.

Civic youth work: Program, practice, and civic youth worker

The three narrative examples suggest, and at times disclose, how civic youth work is done in those contexts, and thus could be done in other spaces and times with young people. The grounded, concrete, particular ways in which it is done are its practices—the civic youth worker embodies knowledge, ethos, craft orientation, and skill. Civic youth work practices are embodied in a (civic) youth worker.

To embody civic youth work is to live these with young people, i.e., do the work in these ways and be this kind of person. This means for us the joining of the correct way to the good and the right in a praxis (all of this is taken up in Chapter Five). To embody and live and be a civic youth worker is to meet each moment with an openness to working in and as and toward democratic ideals and realities with this group of young people here and now. "Here and now" is the spatiotemporal frame in which how the youth worker works discloses the presence or absence of civic youth work. How the workers do the work—how they embody and animate the values, knowledge, skills, and the rest of what we here call youth participation, youth voice, and youth citizenship makes it (or not) civic youth work (as we describe, analyze, and explain in Chapters Four and Five).

Conclusions

These three narrative examples were provided as a taster—a short, insufficiently detailed, and surface introduction to all of the ideas, words, and explanations constituting this primer. As you read, bring each word, each sentence, and idea back to these examples, enriching them with that, as well as with your own experiences as a youth participant and/or as a youth worker, paid or volunteer. Enrich the examples and ennoble them, for in them is Democracy—and that is worth your effort.

So far we have provided theory, concepts, examples, and a bit of discussion. We move next to describing and explicating the doing of civic youth work, and then describe the civic youth worker.

Reflective Questions

1. What commonalities do you see in the three case examples, and do you imagine that these could be universals?
2. What programs, initiatives, and projects have you seen or participated in that you might now name as civic youth work?
3. How does chronological age work as a sociolegal and sociopolitical criterion?
4. What are the everyday, scholarly, and professional biographies of the basic concepts and/or terms designating "youth" in the US, and elsewhere?
5. How do societal age structuring, age segregation, and similar sociocultural, socioeconomic, and sociopolitical structures and practices work to benefit, marginalize, and diminish the social, political, and economic engagement of young people in their society?

Glossary

Ageist: Related to ageism, which is the stereotyping or discriminating against individuals or groups because of their age. This is a concept that is gaining recognition in youth civic engagement to describe the discriminatory policies and programs that view young people as incapable, unable, and without capacity to participate in community change, simply because of their chronological age.

Community social capital: Related to Robert Putnam's ideas of social capital, this concept refers to the strong and weak connections between community members, and is often used to highlight the alienated, isolated, and removed location young people are often provided within communities. Civic youth work addresses this social location, and works to reconnect young people, their ideas, and their issues with others to create a stronger and more vibrant community for all ages.

Disenfranchisement: Refers to the different legal and/or psychological barriers to equal voting and participation in civic processes. In youth civic engagement, it has been proposed as an alternative explanation for young people's low levels of involvement in community and political activities: they live in communities that passively and actively resist their involvement in these types of activities, unless young people participate in adult-sanctioned ways.

United Nations Convention on the Rights of the Child: Ratified by almost every country in the world, except the US and Somalia, this set of rights was created in the late 1980s and was fully implemented in 1990. Countries that ratify the convention are bound to it by international law. While troubling at times for its adult-centered perspective and culture-bound definitions of young person based on chronological age, the convention codifies specific rights for young people, including several that have come to shape the practice and definition of youth participation.

Youth/adult partnerships: A concept created to name collaborative work done in mixed age groups of adults and young people. Concern is on how to balance power within the group so that young people can share in decision-making and have space and time to share their experiences.

Youth citizen: Refers to a field of study and practice that supports young people to be active, thoughtful community participants, change agents, and civic and political contributors.

Youth participation: A form of working with young people that emphasizes listening to them; providing them with decision-making authority; providing choices for what they will do, how they will do it, and when; and clarifying and describing known processes and obstacles so that young people can more effectively make contributions to their communities.

Youth participatory action research: A form of research directly related to participatory action research. This research method supports young people's direct involvement in research in order to create social change that they find personally meaningful.

Youth voice: Often seen as a stance, where young people will not be expected to speak like adults to be listened to; rather, adults and other young people together, will find ways for young people to express what they know and believe, and have these ideas used for program improvement, policy-making, or social change.

4

Doing Civic Youth Work:
The Practice

Civic youth work is a way of working with young people oriented to their becoming and living as citizens who actively engage civic issues and problems meaningful and important to them (if not always consequential for them or them alone). It is a general approach for a collective response to the address of the world as this shows itself as things, conditions, or situations that should be or have to be changed. It is a way to cocreate with young people the answer to the questions of "How should things be better?" It can also answer questions such as, "How shall I live?" and "What is it to be good?" It is an action practice of "how to make the world (school, neighborhood) a better (safer, more interesting) place (to live, work, play, worship . . .). There is neither mystery nor magic in how these are done, while there is great variation in subject, style, and practice.

Basic to democratic youth civic engagement (as we present it) is an adult (or youth) who will take the role of civic youth worker. This means two things: that there is a more or less clear social role that individuals can master, and thus that there is some general similarity in practice across individual practitioners. There is a (small) "community of practice" (Wenger, 1998) in the US and internationally, called variously youth work (Ord, 2007), critical youth work (Belton, 2009), radical youth work (Skott-Myhre, 2006), child and youth care (Stuart, 2012), and more broadly, recreational worker, youth advocate (Dalrymple, 2006), and the like.

Civic youth work practice across and within societies differs in content, but most would agree to the following frame for presentation of the practice: ethos, philosophy and ethics of the work, craft orientation, stance, gaze, knowledge, practices, and skills. One shape for organizing a text can be the interrogatory—questions. This is done by Robbins (2009) in his introduction to anthropology. For example:

- Why do human beings differ in their beliefs and behaviors?
- How do people judge the beliefs and behaviors of others?
- Why did hunter-gatherer societies switch to sedentary agriculture?

A lay source of this is in Leon Neyfakh's (May 20, 2012) piece on questions in the *Boston Sunday Globe* (p. 1), and in Baizerman's (1976) hotline evaluation handbook. It was also the format we have used previously in designing training curricula (VeLure Roholt, McFall, Baizerman, & Smith, 2009), in books on civic youth work (VeLure Roholt, Baizerman, & Hildreth, 2013), and in books on working with youth in contested spaces (Magnuson & Baizerman, 2007). We were inspired by this to include questions at the end of each chapter.

"Steps" in Civic Youth Work Practice

Presented as a logical, abstract process, civic youth work proceeds in 10 steps, which can be divided into four phases or seven stages. Doing actual civic youth work with a group of youth need not follow this sequence. The realities of the individuals, the context and other facts and contingencies prevail, as with all social practice. The 10 steps are:

1. "Something needs to change."
2. "Let's do something about it, together."
3. Understanding what needs to change.
4. Deciding what to do.
5. Figuring out how to do it and rehearsing.
6. Doing it!
7. Celebrating, reflecting on, evaluating, and improving on what was done.
8. What to do next?
9. Working on the issue.
10. Spreading the word.

There is nothing unusual or exotic here; this is simply the classic Western problem-solving model, a Western logical sequence of steps from problem identification to evaluation, and then on to modification, before the cycle begins again. What makes this civic youth work? Why rename this and devote a whole book to it? Answers lie in the purpose of this work and in its practice, how it is done (Chapter Five).

The primary purpose of civic youth work is *not* individual youth development. Yet one of its purposes is the creation and sustentation of social conditions and practices which invite and support this individual development. Good civic youth work practice may enhance the likelihood that a young person's development might be supported by their involvement as a member in a small group of young people who together are working on social change. This assertion comes from two perspectives.

Youth who are active, committed members of a small group of young people working on social change, who chose freely to be part of the group, are likely, in the very process of participating and mastering group roles, to become more competent interpersonally, learn more about a variety of topics, know how to accomplish a variety of tasks, and become more skillful in doing this (VeLure Roholt, Hildreth, & Baizerman, 2008). They are also more likely to have enhanced ethicomoral development if the civic youth work is done correctly, consistently, and long-term (Youniss & Yates, 1997).

In the broader philosophical and empirical frame of human development, in contrast to scientific adolescent development's attention to biophysiological, cognitive, ethicomoral, social, and psychological systematic changes, one's sociopolitical engagement as a citizen is itself a demonstration of enhanced individual development because of the individual's giving of herself to a larger **communitas**. The placing of self into a collective, common pursuit can surely be read developmentally (McIntosh & Youniss, 2010).

What is done, and how it is done—both define civic youth work, its importance, and its uniqueness as a type of work with young people. More abstractly, civic youth work can be summarized from at least two perspectives:

- As a four-phase process.
- As a seven-stage process.

In the four-phase process view, our earliest, focus was on a place or site (VeLure Roholt, Hildreth, & Baizerman, 2008):

1. Entering the place (site).
2. Cocreating the place (site) as a democratic civic rehearsal space.

3. Cosustaining the democratic space at that place (site).
4. Coexpanding the democratic space into the larger world.

These phases seem sequential, and they may turn out to be so, but more importantly, each phase is basic and must be cosustained with the young people over time. Places, sites, and spaces close, and with that, civic youth work can be shut down.

A far richer, more accurate, and more helpful model made distinctions over seven stages (VeLure Roholt, Baizerman, & Hildreth, 2013):

1. Developing group wants and needs.
2. Imagining spaces for group action.
3. Making space by doing the work.
4. Sustaining the space by ongoing work.
5. Evaluating the work.
6. Modifying the practice.
7. Linking the space to larger worlds.

In this view, civic youth work begins with young people with interests and concerns meaningful to them. They come to want "to do something" about this situation, fact, condition, or concern. In their work as a group, they first imagine and make space for their group work. That is, they bring the space into being by their work: they make the road by walking (Horton & Freire, 1990). In Table 4.1 the three frameworks are compared.

Even more abstractly, civic youth work is always the same at the first stage— the beginning, when a group is brought together by a civic youth worker or by the youth themselves through their response to a common issue and/or problem; in the latter, the civic youth worker becomes guide and/or facilitator to individuals with common interests who want to become an action group—i.e., concerned youth. What the civic youth worker does over and over is work democratically with the young people as they move from common interests and concerns to active citizenship through their engagement with issues that matter to them. This is done by ongoing cocreation and cosustentation with the same group of youth, i.e., working with the group as a group, and with individual members as democratic citizens on their movement from interest and concern through analysis and planning to evaluation of their work, and then on to the same issue again, to another issue, to a different bunch of youth who would be a new group, and so on.

Table 4.1. Three Civic Youth Work Frameworks

Four Phases	Seven Stages	Ten Steps
Entering the place (site).	Developing group wants and needs.	"Something needs to change."
		"Let's do something about it, together."
Cocreating the place (site) as a democratic civic rehearsal space.	Imagining spaces for group action.	Understanding what needs to change.
	Making space by doing the work.	Deciding what to do.
Cosustaining the democratic space at that place (site).	Sustaining the space by ongoing work.	Figuring out how to do it and rehearsing.
	Evaluating the work.	Doing it!
	Modifying the practice.	Celebrating, reflecting on, evaluating, and improving on what was done.
Coexpanding the democratic space into the larger world.		What to do next?
		Working on the issue.
	Linking the space to larger worlds.	Spreading the word.

Viewed by an inquiring bird or an airplane passenger, this is what would be seen: a (group) facilitator and a small group talking together. If looked at with one's feet on the ground, and by someone nearby, there is much more to see, analyze, and reflect on.

How to Do Civic Youth Work: The Specifics

Civic youth work always (for us) begins and ends at the same philosophical, ideological, and practical places: with active, intentional, democratic work with individual(s) and small groups of youth **cocreating** and cosustaining their democratic work together on issues of interest, meaning, and concern to them. How is this done? Allowing that every civic youth worker in every context, large and small, will work somewhat differently (and in accord with or in opposition to local sociocultural and political practices and styles), there are similarities. Unfortunately, unlike so much in our lives that is standardized, like a McDonald's burger, the specifics we can offer are a bit less specific and a lot more variable than what is taught in training, or published, or found online in "how to" materials. Even great cooks say a "pinch of salt" and not .237 grams. We offer a more in-depth description and examples from both our own practice and scholarship to further explicate the ten steps introduced earlier.

1. Something needs to change: The very beginning

The very beginning is often named later in the process, because no one really knows who they are or what they are doing at the time when the group first gets started. But let us say they (think they) remember, or an observer was there and saw the beginning.

All of this starts or begins with more or less consciousness that something in one's close to far social world is wrong, and that it needs to be fixed or done better; and that one thinks/feels/believes this, is called/is addressed by this; and comes to feel compelled, and/or to think that one "must do something" about this state of affairs. What could this be? For some individuals in Kansas City, it was the body of a dead cat in front of their school. To many others elsewhere it was school cafeteria food. Many individuals were concerned about school safety and their experiences of danger in local recreation centers and parks. Several wanted their school to provide places for them to play. Quite a few groups wanted to clean up the local park and make improvements to the playground. A few youth thought that there should be information on family planning available in their school and community. Other youth thought that everyone taking a course in the high school should be provided with a textbook they could take home. Several were called to "prevent violence," to confront "poverty," to tackle "world hunger" and child malnourishment, or to respond to child abuse and neglect.

Obviously, some of these were nearby, local issues that mattered to them, while others seemed to be far away, almost untouchable by an individual or even by a youth group. But no: All of these issues/topics/problems/concerns were (phenomenologically and existentially) nearby, touchable to the individual young person thinking, experiencing, and/or feeling that he or she "had to do something" about the reality, and more, that he or she wanted, even needed, to do something: *They experienced a compelling call to act.*

But not always. Some youth did not think or experience or feel such clarity and meaning of interest and/or purpose. They just ended up in a required class which required "service" to their school or larger community. Or their best friends had such vocational clarity and they wanted to stay with them. Or the popular kids were doing it and they wanted to be near those people and have their popularity rub off on them.

And sometimes it was as ordinary as someone saying that some people want to form a group to do something about a problem and want to know who wants to join. And sometimes, a youth worker intentionally brings together a group of young people and tells them what he hears individuals talking about, and asks them if that is important to them. And sometimes a youth worker tells them that this is an issue, and that they should do something about it, and that the youth worker will help.

There are many ways and places in which individual youth come to awareness about and become aware of their beginning commitment to act "to make a difference" in their proximate to distal worlds. In a real and practical sense, it does not matter where the original source of the idea and/or concern comes from. What does matter is that it becomes public, and that at least one youth or civic youth worker feels compelled "to do something" about a real-world problem. Civic youth work begins with this interest made public—talked about with others. How does this interest become public? In a civic youth work act.

An individual's interest can become public when it is said or named, told, and then heard by others, in private or in common space. The civic youth worker has a crucial responsibility at this earliest phase: he or she must constantly ask the youth they are working with whether these are issues/topics/problems/concerns which are meaningful or trouble *them* and which they might want to try to do something about.

This is crucial: Those working with young people must take on this responsibility to constantly ask this ordinary question. *At the moment they see this as their responsibility, a worker or a citizen takes on the role of civic youth worker. When they ask, they are doing civic youth work.* They have taken on a civic youth work ethos and craft orientation.

Phenomenologically, the young person as lived citizen begins here; so, too, **phenomenologically**, does the civic youth work and civic youth worker. For the youth, it begins in the consciousness that something in the world should be different and that oneself is responsible, somehow, "to do something" about it. For the worker, it is their awareness that it is their responsibility to ask and ask and again ask young people whether there is anything in their worlds or in the larger world that they might want to do something about. In so asking, the person is acting as a civic youth worker, *opening the world to possible* individual and collective action. To ask young people about this is to then be responsible for, to be available and present to them if they want to act. From asking to being present and available for working with them on the issue is the architecture, the backbone of civic youth work.

Civic youth work is in being nearby to them, and in doing together with them what becomes their "response" to the address of an issue.

2. "Let's do something about it, together"

Civic youth work becomes more easily visible at this moment, when the work is to move from the individual young person to forming a small group of youth. Here, too, there are lots of ways this is done:

- Worker meets with the young people with the interest/concern and talks about how a group can be more effective in engaging civic issues, theirs and those of others;
- Worker together with that youth recruits others to their work, their cause;
- Youth does this without worker, with friends and others;
- Worker does this without this young person by bringing the issue to others—friends, classmates, neighbors, even strangers.

In our conceptions of democratic youth work practice, the civic youth worker embodies an *invitation to participate* and whenever possible, does so democratically, not coercively, allowing individual young people to decide and to choose whether or not to join. To decide is to make a more or less intellectual selection, while to choose is to existentially commit oneself to the work, the cause. To us, this civic youth work invitation must meet our values test of being open to all, inclusive, and just. To us, *the youth worker goes to young people as a question, not as an answer.* The civic youth worker goes as a particular type of question, a question which invites choice, decision, and action about a world condition.

To "work on this together" means a small group of six, eight, or 10 youth. Many groups begin with fewer or more (and size does not always matter), and some civic youth work in some cultural contexts begins with large groups of 10–20 youth. While more difficult to work democratically with such larger groups, it surely can be done, as seen in the following example.

Public Achievement Northern Ireland, with support from the First and Deputy First Ministries, Community Relations Council, and European Youth Program, organized and facilitated a twelve-day gathering for young civic leaders from twelve regions of the world. The gathering was called simply: Summer Camp. The name was chosen purposively to support the dual-purpose civic education and group cohesiveness and connection. Over 50 young people accepted the invitation. They came from Finland, The Netherlands, Jordan, Croatia, Serbia, Ireland, Northern Ireland, Israel, Palestine, South Africa, the United States, and Turkey, and spent twelve days on the North Coast of Northern Ireland.

An organizing committee met for almost a year prior to the camp to create an overall camp plan. While a daily plan was created, the organizing committee also intended for participants to take over decision-making by the sixth day, realizing that this would dramatically change the plan, if successful. The idea was to plan tight but implement loosely. It did not take six days for the participants to take over; by the third day they had taken over most of the program planning and began to redesign the entire experience.

Two structures created by the organizing committee seemed to facilitate participants' taking over most of the decision-making and redesign. First, all young people were invited to participate in one of six committees: program, evaluation, celebration, media, community, and future directions. These committees were all supported by one of the organizing committee members, and on the first day, participants were told that they could help to make the camp whatever they wanted. Participants quickly accepted the opportunity and responsibility. By the end of the twelve days the different committees had redesigned the entire camp schedule; conducted a mixed-method evaluation of the experience and provided ongoing feedback to the larger group; integrated ongoing social events and celebrations that both highlighted accomplishments by different groups but also increased familiarity between different groups; created a website for ongoing communication after the camp ended that included a monthly newsletter; contacted and secured both local radio and newspaper sources, who completed stories about the camp and individual participants; and created rich cultural programming where everyone learned where people came from, and were introduced to different traditions, foods, and music. The committee structure was supported by daily, whole-group reflections and discussions.

Each morning, all participants gathered to discuss the daily schedule, address issues, and make collective decisions about what they would do and how. As expected, the issue of being "on time" was raised early on in the camp. Finnish participants raised concerns that many of the camp participants continued to arrive late for planned meetings and events. Other participants were perplexed by the comments; from their culture, they were arriving on time to everything, even when this meant they arrived 20–30 minutes after the activity was scheduled. This led to a wonderful conversation about culture and time. While not fully addressed, it raised all participants' understanding of difference. The combination of the committee schedule and daily meetings allowed democratic processes to flourish throughout the twelve days, although it was likely not enough.

What supported ongoing democratic decision-making was an organizing committee that was willing to share power and encouraged participants to take the lead. The structure was important, but not sufficient. For democratic decision-making to flourish required good facilitators willing to address controversial comments and issues when they arose, and who supported participants to take the lead in the overall program; structure was necessary, but so were civic youth workers.

This small (to larger) group is crucial to the civic youth work purpose of cocreating youth citizens, to their lived citizenship, to the creation of ad hoc social action formations, and for social action in democratic civil space. These are "voluntary associations" in the classic de Tocquevillean (1966) sense—citizens freely joining together to present their grievances and/or to try to redress these. It is here where civic youth work moves beyond an individual's voting or sitting as a representative of a youth agency, mayoral committee, or tribal band. Instead, this is **collective work**, a vibrant, necessary (in a civic youth work context), and potentially more effective instrument for change.

The **small group** is the crucible, the training ground, the space for mastery of a significant part of the citizen role—working in a group. It is here where youth can master the basic roles of this social action instrument: leader of or in the group, chair of the group, notetaker, and the rest.

> Group work is one way of training citizens, by offering the experiences that make for constructive citizenship. These experiences are a way of demonstrating that social structure is designed to facilitate the smooth running of society and to protect the rights of the individuals, that minorities have a right to be heard, and that liberty is a priceless heritage. In the agency social club, every voice can be heard and members can see how their voices affect decisions and group thinking. An accumulation of such experience by the members can develop a sense of the value of participation, and an awareness that even one vote in a club can affect the decision on an important matter. Group work aims, also, to develop leadership, and to give members an opportunity to experiment with and practice leadership within their groups (Klein, 1953, pp. 310–311).

The civic youth worker must be a group worker, in both the older, social work sense and way (Konopka, 1963) and in the ways of social-action or social-change

groups (Singh & Salazar, 2011). The two are different in ethos and craft orientation, but are similar in some practices, knowledge, and skills.

Table 4.2. Comparison of Classic and Social-Action Group Work

	Classic Group Work	Social-Action Group Work
Ethos	Collaborative, individual, and group development.	Group development for group action.
Craft Orientation	Working together for individual and group benefit (mutual aid).	Working together to respond to a meaningful public issue.
Knowledge	Group theory and stages of group development, facilitating group.	Developing members' citizen knowledge and skills for engaging an issue publically.
Skills	How to form a group, organize a group, facilitate a meeting, build group agendas.	Selecting, planning, doing, assessing, deciding on next steps, and evaluating what was done.
Practices	Group building, fostering individual and group development.	Issue research, planning civic and political action, ally building, evaluating and planning again, celebrating.

The civic youth worker works with small groups. This is the context, the
space for individual role mastery—of doing and being citizen—both as a person
and also in the citizen role as group member. Most crucial is this group membership, this "being part of," this "working together." However, this may be socioculturally and politically contingent; it is not difficult to imagine (and learn about)
places and situations where group membership enhances danger for both individuals and group. This is surely true in contested spaces (Magnuson & Baizerman,
2007), such as civil conflict and war, and under certain nonviolent, sociopolitical
arrangements, such as working to improve the rights of lesbian, gay, bisexual, and
transgender youth in places throughout the world (Young et al., 2013).
Exacerbating the group-ness of the group is their youth-ness, and when these are
joined in "groups of young people," outside perceptions of them can easily change
from "kids doing stuff together" to "a dangerous youth group" representations of

"youth groups" are quite different than those used to name "young people work-ing together." In several countries, such youth groups are watched closely and active-ly for their seditious potential.

Although the primary purpose of civic youth work is not "healthy individual youth development," nonetheless this may be a consequence of group membership, especially when guided by a skilled civic youth worker. If this occurs—whether in terms of scientific adolescent development or the broader human development—we accept this as a value-added benefit of the civic youth work process.

3. Understanding what needs to change

Beginning at this point, the civic youth worker joins small-group practice to Western (or some other) logics of problem analysis (e.g., Koberg & Bagnall, 1981), decision-making (choosing), planning and evaluation, and corrective action. The civic youth worker is always attentive to how all that happens in and to the group, because the worker and the group's actions contribute at the same time to the young people's mastery of citizen roles, the group's interest in social change, and the pos-sibilities of individual "growth and development." Just as in a rope course where climbing a cliff face with the necessary help of others is metaphoric for trust-making, while allowing for skill (and self) mastery, group activities are what they are—activities toward social change; these can also be read as well as opportuni-ties for the mastery of democratic citizenship.

We do not think that it is necessary to go into detail about these logics, given how easy it is to learn about these (e.g., problem analysis, decision-making, plan-ning, and evaluation). Instead, we focus on how the civic youth worker orients to these logics and processes as citizen-learning metaphors and opportunities.

4. Deciding what to do

It is here that civic youth work can be more clearly described. Civic youth work supports group decision-making. It invites and supports shared understanding among group members of the issues and choices of action, and then facilitates the group, as a group, to decide what they want to do, how, and when. The civic youth worker wants the individual young people to become a group and to work as a group; to make group decisions (Konopka, 1963). In so doing, the group shows to itself that it is a "group," thereby strengthening its "group-ness" for its members. It is in the deciding that democratic practices and democratic citizens can show themselves for what they are—different *embodiments of a lived, democratic ethos;* the young people are both doing democracy and being lived-citizens. Citizenship is also disclosed.

Basic here are small-group process skills, the old "social group work" in social work (Konopka, 1963) and education (Johnson & Johnson, 1975). This is driven by a democratic touchstone of good, right, and correct practice, and the civic youth worker's awareness that it is in inclusive, fair, just, and consequential group decision-making that is found "what citizen is all about."

Decisions are about what issue to work on as a group and why this; then the group must decide on its goal(s).

5. Figuring out how to do it and rehearsing

Once an issue is chosen and goals are set, the group has to figure out how to try to get at the goals. They analyze the interests, forces, power, resources, and authority which can be mobilized by them and by others to achieve and to block achievement of their group goals. Strategy and tactics are considered, and action taken, first in their **rehearsal space**—the small, protected space that they are working in as they work out, and figure out, how to carry out their plan in the larger, consequential world. They practice by talking, deciding, planning, and acting; thinking always about how these will play in the larger, everyday, real world—whether their classroom, school, neighborhood park, community, or other space.

Civic youth work practice is democratic, analytic, reflective, and evaluative, and changes are made in how the issue is understood, their action goals, their plan, strategy and tactics, and in how they will do all of this together. The civic youth worker is guide, coach, teacher, facilitator, mentor, illustrator, actor in role-plays—always making sociopolitical processes for and with the group so that, as a group, they can "work it out"—decide, do—again and again. In so doing, the civic youth worker is cocreating spaces for their discovery of, practice at, and mastery of citizen—the role expectations and lived realities of thinking, being, and doing citizen. This is an experiential pedagogy of democratic citizen-becoming, citizen-making.

All of this is not simply play, simply rehearsing. It is fully about learning, the development of expertise in judgment, action, evaluation, and effort improvement: It is phronetic citizen action, phronetic citizenship, wise-judging and wise-acting.

6. Doing it!

Civic youth work practice is most publically visible when the group and its members do things "out in the open" where their work—their acts and actions—can be seen and heard. When their work is visible, public, and in the name of a public, it is "public work," citizen work, civic work—the practice of democracy.

7. Celebrating, reflecting on, evaluating, and improving on what was done

The civic youth worker leads the group in celebration of its work, their work as a group. And their effort, because they rarely meet with full success the first time they work on their public issue. They rarely achieve their goals: the issue remains, typically. Should they, do they want to continue working on it? In the same ways? What did they do correctly and wrong, and what worked and did not? How can they improve their practice so as to be more effective, more successful—to prevent, control, ameliorate, repair (Spelman, 2003), or otherwise change the world condition they took on? How can they, as a group, become better at the work? And better as a group? Should they simply "pack up their stuff and walk away?" Should they take their marbles or videogames or their friends and "call it quits?"

Civic youth work practice aims at both youth as citizens now and over their lives. In both time frames, these moments of celebration, reflection, evaluation, and ideas for improvement are crucial, because most citizens working in small groups or larger social movements do not meet their goals on the first try, after their first effort. Sometimes this is because many youth groups doing civic engagement in schools or communities are time-bound by the host organization's calendar and schedule. At other times, it may be because the group may take on a difficult, even intractable issue such as "poverty." Given their time, resources, power, and the like, the group very typically does not finish its work—in their terms or in someone else's terms—or they are unsuccessful in that they did not "solve the problem," ameliorate it much, prevent it, or "change the world" as they had hoped and worked toward. However frustrating or painful to the youth and the civic youth worker, this is no surprise to us. Indeed, this often can be read as the work and guidance of a beginning civic youth worker who did not (effectively) insinuate "reality"— likely achievable goals, given "time constraints," into their work with the youth group. Given all of this, and based on the rules and practices of the work settings, the same youth group or individuals from a group may want to continue working on the same issue or on a different one.

If they choose and they decide "to keep at it," to "try again," to get better at the work, to "not give up," then the civic youth worker is a guide through all of this. The civic youth worker has an important role at this moment, helping the group to reflect on their work, and to decide what they want to do next—stop working, or take what they have learned and keep trying to make a difference. Done well, it is more likely that they will "stay with it" and try again to make the world, the river move, as they want it to. Most often, they keep the group going. Why? Because group members want to continue to think and work together and as citizens. How substantively and quickly this group or individuals get at the work and do the work at high quality this second (or third or fourth) time is a good indicator of what they have learned. That is, it is a display, a demonstration, of their mastery of citizen. Doing the group work a second or subsequent time is to watch lived-citizen. For many youth and civic youth workers, the second and third times are far more fun than their first effort. We support young people who want to "keep at it"; this can be a good beginning of lifelong citizen engagement.

Done poorly, the odds are that the young people will go back to their friends, toys, sports, and other pursuits and meanings, leaving citizen work to others. They may feel despondent, frustrated, angry, disillusioned, tired, or whatever. To outsiders, they can look "apathetic" or "bored"; to themselves and to outside viewers both, they are not "citizens." Depending on when they are seen, by whom, where, and how, it may be impossible to see or even imagine their heat, even their flame when they were doing citizen and citizen work. Their citizen-ness will likely be misread.

8. What to do next?

Civic youth work practice is about cocreating spaces for citizen work, doing the work, assessing the work, and improving the work—this time, and next time, and again and again—during youthhood and over a lifetime. In this context, "next" really matters. Knowing that the present is shaped by both its past and its future—by plans, aspirations, goals, and hope—what the group as a group and what individual members want to do next are crucial to them, to how their issue lives in their world, and to their citizen-self.

The civic youth worker works to make all of this explicit, and does so by coleading with young people in the group these reflections, choices, and decisions. This is about "bouncing back," tenacity, "realistic expectations," the motive-power of a compelling interest, one's bonds with the others in the group, and the like. This can be about "maturity," about individual "development," about political wisdom. It is also about being a member of this group.

Some individuals and some groups want to "keep going," to "soldier on," to keep it going.

9. Working on the issue

Individuals can "buy in" again by staying on and staying in the group. The group can continue as the same group, or the group as an issue group can continue and some or all of the current members leave, thus keeping open a space for working on that same issue. Or both the group and the members can be new—even when the issue space seems to be the same. Or . . . we have met young people who have worked on the same issue, and others who have worked on different issues over several years—always learning, always doing, always feeling fulfilled and meaningful, and often experiencing their power and efficacy differently. These young people are far along in their becoming and/or being a citizen. We have seen classroom teachers who have worked as civic youth workers become better at this, and themselves become more a citizen. Their lived-citizen self is more present more often, more richly, and more efficaciously. And we have met and talked with young people who "heard about" the group and its work through a friend or through interest in the issue, and now want to play (Carse, 1987), to "try it out," to become, be, and do citizen.

"And so it goes . . ." (Heller, *Catch 22*).

In these ways, a culture of democratic citizenship can be nurtured in a space like a school, a classroom, a community center, a space of worship, on a sports field, and elsewhere. "Working on" is another way to say that responsibility for making and sustaining enduring democratic work and democratic practice need never end.

10. Spreading the word

Public work, civic work, citizen work is not private. It is about being seen and heard as a group on life conditions which are meaningful and consequential to that group and likely to others, directly or indirectly. It is not solo work, although it may begin as such, with a single young person naming an issue and claiming the right to respond to how this addressed them. The public-ness of this issue and the work is made more noticeable when word of the issue and the work is spread—is public, possibly noisy, even irreverent, at times "radical." Whether by photographs, news stories, videos or voice, face-to-face, and electronically transmitted, produced by the group and/or by others, the civic youth worker has a responsibility to get the word out, a responsibility to do this with young people: a responsibility to the youth in the group, to their work on the issue, to a larger public, to a democratic culture, and to the issue as such. To take and distort from the ethicist, Emmanuel Levinas

(1969), to look the issue straight in its eye is to become responsible for its presence, for its ways of showing itself, for the pain, confusion, and error it brings about. To distort Martin Buber (1958), engaging an issue is to become responsible for its presence and for one's stance and being and living in response to it.

Spreading the word gets at recruiting others to take on, engage the issue, thus beginning again, a civic youth work process and practice.

Working with New Youth on the Same or New Issues

Typically, youth come to work in a group because the issue and/or problem matters to them; the issue is a strong magnet drawing young people into a group. When civic youth work is done in a more or less closed world, such as a school or community center, youth culture or adults in the building can keep alive the issue for another group to take on and own. Here, too, we believe, this is good practice. Important is that the civic youth worker remember that this group of young people are not last year's, and that these youth are not yet a group, and thus the worker must work with them as they are—new, however much the worker knows about both what not and what to do on this issue, as learned "last time."

Conclusions

These ten steps are a kind of "rules of the road." That is, a set of guideposts, not guidelines, for doing and thinking and talking about civic youth work. One of us long ago used a book in New Mexico which told about the rocks, plants, and history mile by mile along each highway in the state. It was like having a curator with you if you wanted to know what was there, whether or not you had noticed or thought about it. What we present is a most incomplete guide, but one fully in that spirit.

Next, we add how to carry out these 10 steps. Some will call these steps civic youth work. No, we say. It is both these steps and how they are walked, are carried out, are done, and named and spoken, that matters. Civic youth work is a praxis of what to do, why, and how to do it. But we do not want to fall into techne, to a list of how the civic youth worker must do specific steps. Each worker must choose these. We have no precise evidence that these steps are scientifically valid and that our proposed ways of doing these steps is more effective. Instead, we have and present below touchstones, places, to learn whether and how a worker is practicing his/her craft, and whether that fits our values, our beliefs, and our sense of how best to do the work. This is not science, mind you; this, at best, is judgment which may rise to the level of practical wisdom—phronesis (again).

Reflective Questions

1. Should civic youth work be thought of as civic adolescent work, and why (not)?
2. Can someone with a sociological or anthropological or dental or no formal education do civic youth work, and do it as well as a trained, semi-professional youth worker?
3. In what ways does (not) civic youth work meet the scholarly test of (being) a practice?
4. For you, is civic youth work best understood in a (neo)positivist, interpretive, practical science, or mixed frame, and why?
5. Is "citizen making" being accomplished through civic youth work if it is not named as such?

Glossary

Cocreating: A way of working with (young) people grounded in human science and phenomenological philosophy. An orientation to cocreation assumes that young people often understand differently the world they share with adults. Cocreating begins by first learning from the young person who they are, and then working to open up a collaborative and creative space to share ideas, concerns, and questions.

Collective work: Work done together to achieve a joint, agreed-upon goal.

Communitas: Latin. Refers to the feeling of significant and intense community spirit, togetherness, belonging.

Phenomenologically: Work grounded in the Continental philosophy of phenomenology. Phenomenology attends to the everyday experiences of others, and uses these to make choices, in this way moving to more deeply understand people and what they are capable of doing.

Rehearsal space: The small, protected space that is created to work through and work out ideas and ways of responding, so that individuals and groups can master styles and content, and process and prepare final action to carry out in the larger, consequential world.

Small group: More than a group of individuals, a small group becomes a unit in itself. Members work together so that everyone's talents are noticed, named, and put to use, and individual weaknesses matter less.

5

Civic Youth Work:
The Practice of Civic Youth Work(er)

The second constituent of civic youth work is its practice (Higgs, Titchen, & Neville, 2001): the concrete, particular ways a specific worker does civic youth work, general guidelines and touchstones of civic youth work practice, and what it is like to be and to do civic youth work—the practitioner, the doer.

We ask the reader to remember the case narrative presented in Chapter One, current work in St. Paul, Minnesota, by coauthor, Ross VeLure Roholt. We read this work again to get at how conceptions of youth, citizen, and youth work are made real in the everyday doing of civic youth work. Then we step back, and in short essays explore this practice and then the practitioner. By the end of this chapter, the reader should be well-enough acquainted with the three constituents of civic youth work—project, practice, and practitioner—to be addressed by a substantial chapter on evaluating civic youth work.

We hone in closely to examine practice from an emergent perspective, reenergized from its earlier Greek and Aristotelian sources: phronesis and praxis.

As Ethos, Craft Orientation, Practices, and Skills

Civic youth work can be understood analytically and practically as being constituted by an ethos, a craft orientation, knowledge, skills, and practices. An **ethos** of a practice is its philosophical sources and philosophical stance—analytically and practically, in that the ethos (should) guide practice theoretically and in everyday work. The civic youth worker ethos is constituted by three sets of ideas: an anthropology of human being and of youth, a sociopolitical philosophy, and a philosophy of practice. Here, the core is a philosophical (or theological or political) anthropology, for example, human being as political—Homo politicus. Anthropology of human being is the philosophical conception of person, rather than the scientific conception or image of the human (Friedman, 1972). Second is a social (political, economic, and related) philosophy, a conception of how the world could be and is (that is not scientific—not from sociology, political science, or anthropology, etc.). Third is a philosophy of practice; a conception of what the work is and how it is to be done.

In civic youth work, the base is an image of youth as capable and as available to be invited into joint action with others on issues which are meaningful to them (Checkoway, Richards-Schuster, et al., 2003). Ours is not a developmental image, although we do not deny this or its heuristic utility or scientific truth. We conceive of civic youth work grounded elsewhere: an embodied **capability (approach)** (Biggeri, Ballet, & Comim, 2011) and interest awaiting a call or address to become engaged, mobilized, and activated meaningfully. Our social philosophy is grounded in citizen development and citizen engagement; we do not age-grade this practice. Indeed, while we agree with a capability approach to working with and understanding young people (Ballet, Biggeri, & Comim, 2011), we do not want to intentionally or unintentionally reify age, using it as a proxy for describing capacity, capability, or talent. What a person can do is connected to their physical development and their experiences, but neither of these correlates well with age (Lansdown, 2005). Civic youth work practice is grounded in values which give it sources and guidance both, such that the practice is inclusive, just, and nonviolent.

Our philosophy of practice, as will be described, is derived from Aristotle's **phronesis**—practical wisdom and judgment, not largely or only technological rationality. We believe that technique as such can become an illusion (Barrett, 1979). We work in ways emergent, situational, responsive to the moment, as if playing improvisational jazz and not dancing classical Russian or American ballet. In the latter, one practices and practices to get it right, while in the former one practices and practices so as to be able to do what one has to do and/or what has to be done, when and how that must and/or should be done. We work to join the technically correct to the morally good and the ethically right (source) in each moment (Benner, 1994). This is civic youth work's craft orientation. This is civic youth work practice. Civic youth worker skill is making this work more often than not. That is civic youth work expertise (Dreyfus & Dreyfus, 1991).

All of this, we assert, is what makes up civic youth work practice. When embodied, all of this becomes the civic youth worker. When all of this is made real, concrete, particular, and specific, it is **lived practice**. The worker and the practice come together in a praxis of one—the work and the worker become the same. The next section takes up this notion by examining how the work, the worker, and the practice are joined.

Joining the Work, the Practice, and the Person in How the Work Is Done

This praxis of work, worker, and practice becomes real and actual and not simply analytic in a concrete, specific, particular moment. This is where and when doing and being emerge. It can begin with thinking and perceiving.

Perceiving as a civic youth worker: Stance and gaze

Much of civic youth work is activated in perception. A civic youth worker takes a civic youth work stance—a position—in relation to youth (in general, and with the particular young person he or she is working with); that young person must be invited by them or others to be actively involved on issues which matter to the youth. The civic youth worker and others act to open spaces for civic youth work, and the worker and others support the young people when they enter and use this space (VeLure Roholt, Baizerman, & Hildreth, 2013).

In that stance, the civic youth worker takes on and uses a particular gaze. In viewing ordinary, mundane, everyday life, the civic youth worker sees, senses, and/or imagines:

- Potential space for beginning mastery of (being and doing) citizen.
- The young people as citizens.
- The possibilities of and/or in the potential space.
- Where and how to begin (artistry).
- The potential of each group member.
- Each group member as a citizen-becoming.
- How the issue they care about can be worked (on).

Put differently, the worker literally sees five or eight teenagers in a room. But the worker perceives them as "citizens"—becoming (a more activated or animated state than young people with citizen potential). They are already on their way to becoming "citizens." Beyond their perception, the worker senses where and how to grasp an issue interesting and meaningful to young people, here and now. This is the worker's civic youth work craft knowledge, based on his or her experience working as a (civic) youth worker.

They know what they want to try: Expertise

On expertise, we prefer Dreyfus and Dreyfus's account (1991), among the many hundreds of substantive analyses (Ericsson, 2006). Their model is comprised of seven stages of expertise: Novice, Advanced Beginner, Competence, Proficiency, Expertise, Mastery, and Practical Wisdom (Dreyfus, 2001).

This model recognizes the joining of technique to values in practical wisdom—phronesis. Civic youth work is valuational and ideological in its commitments to change on the micro (e.g., Zukin, Keeter, Andolina, Jenkins, & Delli Carpini, 2006), mezzo (e.g., O'Donoghue & Kirshner, 2008), and macro (e.g., Gordon, 2010) levels in the name of social justice, inclusiveness, and democratic participation. Dreyfus & Dreyfus (1991) also clearly differentiated levels of expertise, and did not simply use a dichotomous nonexpert/expert distinction; it is useful for preparing civic youth workers and citizens, and for evaluating civic youth work initiatives.

Table 5.1 shows what we consider to be the levels of civic youth worker expertise.

Workers with a civic youth work stance can literally see, as well as perceive, sense, and imagine how in any particular here and now, they might work with these particular young people on their chosen issue. The civic youth worker "knows" what might work here and now, with these specific youth. This is partly their experience and partly their wanting to try (and willingness to try) their idea of what to do and why. They are wanting and willing to figure out how to do this work together in a series of how "we try this together." The civic youth worker's expertise lies in the joining of a knowing what might be done, what is wanted, a willingness to try it, a knowing how to do it and how to get it done.

If a civic youth worker tries something, and you as observer ask them what they did and why they did this, they might say:

Table 5.1. Levels of Civic Youth Work Expertise

Stages of Expertise	Dreyfus Description	Civic Youth Worker
Novice	Novice learns decontextualized and simplified rules to determine action.	Civic youth work is rule-bound, often working from curricula and guidebooks with step-by-step directions of what to do and how to do it.
Advanced Beginner	The advanced beginner "gains experiences," and recognizes aspects that only appear in context. They develop maxims, which combine situational aspects with general rules to take action.	Civic youth worker becomes experienced and begins to read young person contextually and situationally, developing "rules of thumb" and other guides which get at the moment and join this to general rules of when and how to act.
Competence	Worker gains more experience, and encounters a large number of examples that do not fit well with the rules. He or she develops choice of actions based on hierarchal frameworks.	Civic youth worker has enough experience to know when and how to best work with a young person to facilitate his or her development as a citizen.
Proficiency	The worker knows what to do given the complexity of the situation, but not always how to do it. He or she can figure out what to do and move towards intuitive reactions.	Civic youth worker knows what action to take but not always how to do this; has knowledge to work this out and some intuition on what to do.
Expertise	"What must be done, simply is done" (Dreyfus, 2001, p. 42). They see what needs to be done, and immediately sense how to achieve this goal.	Civic youth worker is a "jazz musician," cocreating with group of young people the whole issue-based, social-action process, without giving much thought to the process or to how to act in each moment with each young person.
Mastery	Work out own style of the work, no longer simply copy, but now create their own unique way of doing the work.	Civic youth worker develops his or her own ways of doing the work, building from their talents, skills, and interests, while doing the work grounded in relevant ethos, purpose, and outcome.
Practical Wisdom	"The general ability to do the appropriate thing, at the appropriate time, in the appropriate way" (Dreyfus, 2001, p. 48).	Civic youth worker deeply embodies democratic ways of being and doing, and brings this about in almost any context, fostering these in others.

- "This is how I work with young people."
- "This is how I work on issues like this one."
- "This is how I work with young people like this on issues like this."
- "Oh, this is just civic youth work."
- "Oh, given my experience with youth like these, and working on this issue or similar ones, I typically try to . . ."

These sentences get at civic youth work accounts (Scott & Lyman, 1968)—what civic youth workers tell about what was done, how, and why. These may be interesting, inaccurate, incomplete, or simply "just talk." **Reflective practice**, to be said right, fully, and well requires a relevant, appropriate language, and concepts, and ways of telling—appropriate narratives (Schon, 1983): the right kind of story must be told. Civic youth work must learn how to tell these right and good stories—stories that teach, show, and explain in their telling. Needed, too, is a civic youth work language, to name the work and/or practice so that it can be heard and seen as such.

Doing the Work

Taking an intentional stance and gazing at young people are some of the ways of doing the work. There are others:

- Knowing each youth as who he or she is and as citizen-becoming;
- Cocreating with young people a small youth group;
- Figuring out with the group its structure and ground rules for selecting and working together on an issue;
- Teaching about and doing the processes which, while working on the chosen topic, are the opportunities to come to know, try out, assess, and refine aspects of the citizen role—ways of perceiving, analyzing, reflecting, deciding, organizing, arguing, convincing, mobilizing, acting, and the rest;
- Doing all of this as group member, leader, researcher, advocate, evaluator, and the like—citizen roles with citizen knowledge, attitudes, values, and skills.

It is the civic youth worker's job to be available to guide all of this with, and if necessary, on behalf of the group. When done correctly, this is a politico-learning process using an experiential (Kolb, 1984) and a **critical pedagogy** (Kincheloe, 2008), in educational terms. In political terms, it is a space for mastering the citizen role, of becoming and being citizen (VeLure Roholt, Hildreth, & Baizerman, 2008). Along the way and always, the civic youth worker names what is going on in several languages—everyday, idiomatic English (or Spanish, or Lakota, or . . .)—in citizen terms, in the terms of "public work" (Boyte & Farr, 1997) and civic life. When appropriate and requested, this is named in academic concepts such as social capital, social role, and power. Of course, the civic youth worker also solicits and uses the youths' language(s) for what is going on: civic youth work is multilingual and multivocal. Again, much of this is normative in the West and North, and while there are some logics more widely used and easily accessible, there are many which are used locally, and are not widely well-known, but make sense and are legitimate in local contexts: there is not one way and none of this is exotic. But it is important—do not confuse the two.

How is the work done? Touchstones of practice

There are at least two ways to get at the how of civic youth work, how civic youth work is done: technique-driven (techne) and ethos-driven (phronesis). We use the ethos-guided way of practice.

The worker practicing in the civic youth work ethos-guided way has a general approach, "a way," that is given specificity within each concrete, particular moment (Friedman, 1972). That means that the worker constantly assesses and judges what to do in each situation. He does not simply "apply" the same technique each time, responding to each young person and each group the same or even uniquely. He discerns, differentiates, distinguishes similarities and differences, and acts accordingly. This is obvious, but we all have had the experience of being a widget to a practitioner who treats us as if we were just like the last person he or she treated and neither sees us nor responds to us in our uniqueness (Orange, 2010).

Ethos-guided work is grounded in "a way" (Mayeroff, 1971), and that way is grounded partly in values—what is of value and/or worth, what matters, what is meaningful. These values can be treated as **touchstones**—places, ideas, and beliefs that test the rightness, goodness, and correctness of what the worker wants to do and how the worker will carry this out:

> Along with its other connotations, the word "touchstone" suggests probing, testing, proving—but in an existential sense; that is, as something we take back with us into the new situation that we meet. It helps us relate to that new situation, but the situation also modifies the touchstone. On us is laid the task, as long as we live, of going on probing, proving, testing, authenticating—never resting

content with any earlier formulations. However true our touchstone, it will cease to be true if we do not make it real again by testing it in each new situation (Friedman, 1972, p. 24).

In this view, the civic youth worker approaches an individual young person before he or she is a member of a youth group as a "possible member." The worker goes toward the youth as an "invitation to join" (others to work together on an issue). What the worker actually says is not a worked-out spiel, the same words said to every young person approached. he or she knows the basic message and improvises with each young person. Totally obvious!

And extremely important for how civic youth work is (to be) practiced. Invisible and not easily discerned in this example is a working touchstone, an integrated, inextricable complex of civic youth work practice, civic youth worker, and moment. Here the touchstone is: the worker is an embodied, ongoing invitation to participate (and to do so) democratically. It is this way—how the civic youth worker practices—that joins civic youth work practice to (the) young person and to the worker: the civic youth worker practicing is their lived ethos.

A second touchstone is also valuational: the workers are is an embodied, ongoing invitation to always work democratically, and in ways just, inclusive, nonviolent, and transparent. They are part of the group, but not necessarily the "leader" or "facilitator." As in other participatory work, civic youth workers "carry the leadership baton lightly and are willing to let it pass from hand to hand" (Wren, 1977, p. 21). Their role is fluid, and cocreated with young people throughout the process, with the primary focus on demonstrating democratic ways of working— inviting and encouraging young people to take on new roles, to cocreate with them—to be citizens.

In practice, this can take many forms but remains grounded in listening and learning—in dialogue (Buber, 1958). The practice "becomes a dialogue in which everyone knows something but is ignorant of something else, and all strive together to understand more" (Wren, 1977, p. 13). Civic youth workers figure out how to cocreate a democratic and engaging space with young people. This space becomes political when the group together begins to name and choose to act on public issues.

A third touchstone is that the worker is an embodied, ongoing invitation to work democratically on issues the participating young people find meaningful and consequential. Too often, young people are cast as apathetic and disengaged (Males, 1996). Civic youth workers approach young people as having interest in and desire to work on public issues. Over the course of ten years, we have not met many young people who did not have at least one public issue they found personally meaningful. The civic youth worker invites young people, through both their actions and words, to name and discuss public issues that they care about and may want to engage. These are more than public issues, but disclose who young people are and what they imagine their future to be.

Civic youth work works with young people to understand who they are, what they want to do, together and alone, and figures out ways these can be done now. Being open to valuing the input from young people involves not simply hearing a set of ideas or views; rather, it involves connecting with the whole "experience" of that person's world, and appreciating the significance of that view or experience in the context of their life (Percy-Smith, 2012, p. 18).

Civic youth work begins when the group recognizes the connection between a public issue and their own lives. These issues are not something they have to work on; rather, these issues connect to and emerge from who they are—the experiences they have had, the history they hold true, and the future they want to create. When this occurs, a young person is "addressed" (by that issue); how they "respond" is who they are.

A fourth touchstone is: the worker is an embodied, ongoing invitation to work democratically with young people, involving them always in individual and group choice, decision-making, analysis, action, evaluation, reflection, and improvement of the work. Civic youth workers do not make decisions for a group; instead they build group members' capacity to collectively decide what they will do, how, when, where, and who will do what, and then they together evaluate what they did. Civic youth workers build "choice space[s], instead of making choices for [young people], in such a manner that rational and reasonable decision-making is favored" (Ballet et al., 2011, p. 27). The worker supports the group to make intentional choices about how to move the work forward, and questions the group about whether or not these choices are made in democratic, inclusive, nonviolent, just, and deliberate ways.

This connects to the fifth touchstone: the worker is an embodied, ongoing invitation to work democratically, doing so in ways cocreative and cosustaining, and always sharing power with the group.

A sixth touchstone: the civic youth worker works with young people to together cocreate spaces, and uses practice for the ongoing movement of willing youth to develop from young person to citizen to lived citizen(ship). He or she creates active citizen space:

In the course of democratic movements, as a people move into action, they change. They discover in themselves and in their ways of life new democratic potentials. They find out new political facts about the world. They build networks and seek contacts with other groups of the powerless to forge a broader group identity. In turn, for such processes to occur requires more than local, communal roots. Such spaces must also be relatively autonomous, free from elite control (Evans & Boyte, 1986, p. 188).

Having autonomous space is difficult to do in adult, democratic movements; it is especially challenging to create and sustain in youth spaces. Young people often are not allowed to work outside of elite control; indeed, youth programs are often created for the express purpose of control, and even liberal instruments, such as the Convention on the Rights of the Child, have been found to focus primarily on control, even with several protocols calling for greater participation (Ballet et al., 2011).

A seventh touchstone: the civic youth worker attends to whether and how each youth is addressed or called to an issue and to citizen work, and cocreates spaces with each to respond, to discern, to live as that person (vocation). Civic youth work orients both to those who are addressed by the world and want to respond to that call, and to those who discern no such compelling claim on their interests. With the former the work is easier, at least at first, simply because the person wants to "do something"; the task is to move with that individual, joining them to others. The operative question is how to best do this, given the individual, their interests, and others with whom they could work.

In contrast, the civic youth worker has more to do when working with individuals who experience neither a call to "get involved" nor an issue which "grabs them." Here the civic youth worker must move with the young person from wherever they are, to considering their own engagement, then to realizing this for their issue of interest and concern, then to choosing to work on one of these, then to joining with others to actually do the work. The first issue of civic youth work is how to work with young persons so that they are willing to consider both an issue and their possible engagement; this is youth work, mostly, with some civic youth work around how an issue can invite, address, or call an individual to consider it and themself—as a person and as a possible civic activist. If that is too big a change, consider oneself as someone who is aware of an issue that matters to them, and that matters enough so that they will consider "doing something" about it.

An eighth touchstone: the civic youth worker is like the Weber's ideal-type (Hekman, 1983) youth worker in the joining of thought and action, using as

knowledge what is at hand and what is in the tradition of democratic civic practice: the young people participating, the local community and its worlds, and scholarship. Civic youth work is not mere "action"—it is thoughtful (group) action. Civic
youth workers support praxis, the joining of reflection and action to a moral
ground. They work to avoid both verbalism (getting stuck in talking about what
the group is going to do), and activism (acting without thought or consideration
of alternatives and consequences) (Freire, 1970).

Much current youth civic engagement supports verbalism. Youth groups and
facilitators talk at great length about what they want to do and should do, but never
move into doing it! It seems we enjoy watching kids simulate exercises with the
understanding that they are learning. Hart (1992) would describe these participatory projects as either tokenistic or decorative. We are less comfortable with young
people acting on public issues, especially in a public way. When young people
choose to act, their actions are often scrutinized for what adults would call signs
of being "immature" or "naïve." We want young people to act in private, yet social
and political participation "is a visible action in public" (Comim, Ballet, Biggeri,
& Iervese, 2011, p. 12). Civic youth workers support young people's inclusion in
social and political participation, i.e., in public work (Boyte & Farr, 1997).

A ninth touchstone: the civic youth worker works in a democratic, nonviolent,
just, and inclusive tradition and for an organization, forever attentive to and
responsible to both the young people they serve and to the tradition, never exploit-
ing one or the other. The civic youth worker must know where they themselves
stand on issues of practicing democratically; on their willingness and comfort to
work on often contentious, difficult, or conflictual topics; their own "take" on the
issue the youth group has chosen; and the potential tensions, difficulties, conflict,
and related job security difficulties; many civic youth workers love their jobs, get
pulled away from this work, or burn out doing it because their employer "will not
go there." The agency, school, or organization administration will not allow young
people a voice or "has issues" with the topic the young people chose and want to
(are) working on, or are themselves pursued by their constituencies, or the like.

The final touchstone: the civic youth worker, as an embodiment of democratic, civic practice, is responsible for how they disclose in their work this tradition
and culture. This is their deepest pedagogy—a democratic way of living, being, and
doing. The civic youth worker's lived self (van Manen, 1990) and lived practice
must embody his or her ongoing invitation to the young people to see themselves
as, to be as, and to work together as democratic citizens. At its base, civic youth
work practice is an experiential pedagogy (Kolb, 1984) where young people learn
by talking, doing, and discussing what they did—a "reflective practice" (Schon,

1983). This links directly to their lived self. The civic youth worker's lived self, their lived body, lived time, lived space, and lived relationships (van Manen, 1990) are phenomenologically democratic; are experienced by the workers themselves as "I am doing citizen in how I am and how I work with these young people, here and now." By "doing citizen," they (become) are citizen: being follows doing, in the classical U.S. model of self-in-action. Said differently, they become their (democratic) practice, phenomenologically speaking.

Practicing Ethos—Animating Civic Youth Work

The ten lived touchstones come from practice, and from scholarship. We have called them touchstones and asserted their animating and grounding presence in how civic youth work is lived, practiced, and carried out. This list is not catechismic, nor is it universal across history, place, and cultures. It is one way to continue the conversation about civic youth work as a practice, about the civic youth worker role, and the adult civic youth worker as person.

The Convention on the Rights of the Child, the Universal Declaration of Human Rights, and other international instruments assert their universality and engender conflict because of this. Challenged are deeper foundational, philosophical, theological, or sociopolitical anthropologies of human beings and human society: Who has sociopolitical legitimacy to assert "on behalf of humankind?" We are neither that arrogant, nor ambitious; rather, we want to explicate a democratic value nexus which we believe can and does underlie civic youth work (at its best). Surely, there are other models, other values, other practices, and other ways to get at and to present alternative frames and conceptions of civic youth work. Those we leave to our colleagues and fellow citizens; that task is yours for the taking.

Being a civic youth worker: How do the pieces fit?

Being a civic youth worker in our frame is braided with doing civic youth work as a civic youth worker: These are of a whole. Atomists prefer analytic distinctions which parse elements of one from the others. That is easier than telling exactly how each contributes to the other. When the civic youth worker is practicing, he or she is reciprocally intertwined in time: ask any potter, weaver, jazz musician or barber (Bensman & Lilienfeld, 1973). In the end, expertise may be visible, identifiable, categorizable, and ultimately elusive; at least for now, and at least for here. Civic youth work does not have a punch line—a simple "here it is, master it, go forth." Rather, it is a way of being and doing; of seeing, thinking, and acting.

Metaphors For Civic Youth Work

Metaphors can make visible a phenomenon or practice little noticed (Lakoff & Johnson, 2003). Civic youth work, when done well, is like athletic precision and beauty, seemingly simple, so easy that "even a young person could do it." Making work seem easy can be a sign of expertise, the flow of doing by a master—athlete, potter, musician, car mechanic, even a youth worker! Among the many metaphors of civic youth work which make visible and intelligible this mundane work are the following; the list is only a taster.

- Builder

  A civic youth worker builds small groups by bringing together individuals, and working to construct from and with them as a group, not simply as a collection of persons. The skills to do this lie in the "forging" of interdependencies among individuals who became group members.

- Conductor

  A civic youth worker can be thought of as conductor of a group working on an issue in a more or less explicit process. This view presumes a musical score with notes, tempo, instrumentation, and the rest. Misleadingly, there may be no musical and/or procedural score, only general guidance about where to begin and try to get to. Civic youth work may be more improvisational jazz than Bach or formal ballet; all need conductors, but their skills differ, as do ethos, craft, knowledge, and practices. Here the worker, in a pun, must know the score.

- Guide

  Civic youth workers are guides, in the wilderness for those new to group civic action, and on formal trails for young people experienced in group action. Guide and guidance are important metaphors to understand civic youth work, because this metaphor highlights the responsibilities of both guide and hiker, and their interdependency. Here the workers (sort of) know where they are heading, if not where they are going.

- Facilitator

  Civic youth workers facilitate small groups of young people working on civic issues as citizens. Emphasis here, too, is on the role of each which together "makes things work." Again, interdependency. Here the worker's praxis is group process.

- Coach

  So, too, with coach. Expertise here is a strategic vision—knowledge about different group roles, players' skills and temperaments, and tactics. Coaches know about and can teach how to.

- Lighthouse

  Civic youth workers work as high-intensity light beams for groups that want and/or need to find direction, to avoid dangerous shoals which likely cause disaster; they help travelers get to their destination safely. Civic youth workers are such beacons, such foghorns, such preventive light and noise to or for an activist youth group.

- Consultant

  Civic youth workers are both in or of, and out or marginal to the group. They belong to it, however different their membership roles compared to those of the young people. They advise, cajole, facilitate, coach, and also in these roles, consult, always leaving choices and decisions to the youth (except when safety, inclusiveness, social justice, and similar core values are at stake). When core values are threatened, civic youth workers become players, different, not equal, the voice of age, authority, expertise, and moral standards. All of this is clear and direct conceptually, but subtle and complex in practice.

These seven metaphors playfully disclose what civic youth work is and how it is positioned and works. It is an illustrative, not definitive, beginning.

Conclusions

Civic youth work as an orientation and a practice can be done wherever and/or whenever a pedagogic place (Foran & Olson, 2008) can be found, or, as in the subtitle of our earlier book on civic youth work (VeLure Roholt, Baizerman, & Hildreth, 2013), wherever and/or whenever such spaces can be cocreated with young people. We quoted there this Spanish proverb: *Se hace camino al andar.* You make the road by walking it. In civic youth work practice, workers and young people together bring a workspace into being through their work—their walk. Such spaces may not be "the right place" (Foran & Olson, 2008, p. 24), or the best place for civic youth work pedagogy, but in a pragmatic sense, it is a space wherein worker and young person can work together. Remember that both metaphorically and in practice, such cocreated, democratic spaces can be opened, and these surely can close, requiring new spaces to be opened by young people and workers. This is a broad-stroke overview of the civic youth worker—abstractly presented. What remains is to show this concretely. This we do in the next chapter.

Reflective Questions

1. Is civic youth work more an identifying label than a practice, more a perspective than either of those, more a language than any of these?
2. What is the place of young people in conceptualizing and practicing civic youth work?
3. Can civic youth work be done with young people seen as difficult by family, school, or community?

Glossary

Capability (Approach): A focus on human beings (of all ages) and what they can be and do in leading a valuable life (regardless of age).

Critical pedagogy: A philosophy of education described by Henry Giroux (2010) as an "educational movement, guided by passion and principle, to help students develop consciousness of freedom, recognize authoritarian tendencies, and connect knowledge to power and the ability to take constructive action."

Ethos: Greek word that translates as *character*. Used to describe the defining belief or ideals of something, in this case civic youth work or a youth organization/agency.

Lived practice: Grounded in phenomenology and hermeneutic phenomenology, refers to the way one personally experiences what they are doing and for what purpose. Usually includes four aspects: lived body (how one experiences their own physical body), lived time (does time fly by or crawl?), lived space (experienced as expansive or constricted, for example), and lived others (partners, students, allies, etc.).

Phronesis: Greek work that translates as *wisdom*. Used to describe a highly skillful form of practice, one that constantly strives to join the technically correct to the morally good and the ethically right (source) in each moment.

Reflective practice: The capacity to reflect on action to support continuous learning.

Touchstone: A stone which is used to test the purity and quality of another stone. It is a stone of known quality against which others are tested. For us, these refer to the shape and form of doing civic youth work that brings about a particular ethos. It is the spirit of the practice that works to support a democratic space for young people.

6

Evaluating Civic Youth Work

It is now common to require the evaluation of youth civic engagement programs, projects, and initiatives, and to urge its use for program improvement, account-ability, and policy and program decision-making. This is a relatively new state of affairs. Thirty years ago, such efforts were taken to be valuable on their face, and little systematic, funded, practical, and/or professional evaluation was done. This was true even though it was known then that evaluation was a good, practical, rel-atively low-cost research strategy for practical programmatic change and other uses. There is now a vast scholarly and professional structure in several fields for train-ing evaluators, and a voluminous literature on evaluation philosophy, theory, practice, and findings. Here, we offer only a short, cursory introduction to eval-uation, and then move quickly to a distinction between program evaluation and evaluation of a practice, such as civic youth work. With a quick nod to how eval-uation in its essence is a political practice, we move to the place, foci, approach-es, and guidelines for evaluation in the field of civic youth work.

What Is Evaluation?

Uncommon in the 1960s, and increasingly typical, even required of youth pro-grams and services, especially when receiving public or foundation support, is a formal evaluation of the work. What is evaluation? Mattessich's (2003) definition is a useful one:

> Evaluation is a systematic process for an organization to obtain information on its activities, its impacts, and the effectiveness of its work, so that it can improve its activities and describe its accomplishments. (p. 3)

As with all formal inquiry, evaluation is a systematic process to insure accurate, trustworthy, and reliable data, reducing bias to make more likely true findings. For our purposes, notice the focus of evaluation on its uses—program improvement and better descriptions of program accounts. Evaluation is a practical enterprise, used to document, explore, and assess in the practical, everyday world of actual practices and programs (Weiss, 1998).

While Mattessich's definition emphasizes "program" as the unit of analysis, this can be easily adapted for the evaluation of practice. By including practice as a focus, this broadens and deepens the definition of evaluation to include practitioners and young people. The definition enriched by use for our purposes becomes:

> Evaluation is a systematic process by which an organization, practitioner, and participating youth obtain information on its (their) activities, its (their) impacts, and the effectiveness of its (their) work, so that it (they) can improve what is done, describe its (their) accomplishments, and in other ways contribute to agency, program, workers, and young people.

Evaluation is about decision-making; it is concerned with judging merit or worth (Rossi, Freeman, & Lipsey, 2003); it is more than simply learning about programs. "It also involves deciding if these programs are worthwhile for young people, their communities, and society" (VeLure Roholt, Hildreth, & Baizerman, 2008, p. 73). Evaluation is about "social betterment" (Mark, Henry, & Julnes, 2000) in all its moral, cultural, and historical complexities. Such assessments are, in effect, if not always consciously so in practice, political. Indeed, evaluation is a political process of locating, documenting, and assessing programs (Weiss, 1998).

By rewriting that evaluation is to include young people and practitioners, we made the political essence of evaluation visible. Evaluation is a political activity, in that it is a valuing activity. This brings us to what is assigned value, by whom, and how? For example, do we care more about whether young people learn facts about governance, or whether they are active and involved in democratic, community, and social development?

This expanded conception of evaluation opens questions about evaluation and its practice. For example, is it best to hire an external evaluator, who can remain objective to the process, or is there more value in conducting a "**participatory evaluation**" (Cousins & Earl, 1995; Sabo Flores, 2008)? Who decides how activities will be described? Will activities simply include what can be observed, or do we want to know how participants make sense of their experience? Who is committed (and not) to using an evaluation study for improvement? Can an evaluation report not be used? Who decides what will be evaluated, and how this will be done? How can the use of an evaluation study be enhanced? These questions open up the spaces between and among evaluation, the larger sociopolitical process of programs and practices, and social (behavioral) and other schools of research (Mathison, 2008).

Practice and Program Evaluation

The evaluation literature focuses primarily on program and policy evaluation, with a few exceptions (Gitlin & Smyth, 1989; Rogers & Williams, 2006). Both program and practice evaluations use the same research methods (qualitative, quantitative, or mixed methods). This is where similarities end. Somewhat obviously, the unit of analysis, approach, and desired results can differ significantly. Program evaluation emphasizes decision-making, accountability, policy-making, and program improvement; while practice evaluation emphasizes ongoing learning, adaptation, and raising practice quality (Rogers & Williams, 2006). Program evaluation includes participatory approaches as an option, while in practice evaluation, participatory approaches are preferred. Evaluating practice cannot be based on external and universal understandings, because it focuses on describing both what practitioners actually do and how they understand what they did (Gitlin & Smyth, 1989). A major tension in evaluating a practice is to understand both what practitioners have done and their understanding of their practice decisions (Gitlin & Smyth, 1989). Evaluation can even go a step further and ask critical reflective questions, such as, "Should this work be done at all?" These distinctions between program and practice evaluation are seen in Table 6.1. Both evaluation foci can be employed in understanding youth civic engagement and civic youth work.

Table 6.1. Comparing Practice and Program Evaluation

Evaluation	Practice	Program
Unit of Analysis	Practice—what staff do and how.	Program—what is delivered to "clients."
Methods	Various; "scientific."	Various; "scientific."
Approach	Often participatory.	Typically externally designed study.
Result	Ongoing learning. Practice adaptation. Raising worker quality and thus quality of service.	Accountability. Decision-making. Policy-making. Program improvement.

Evaluating Youth Civic Engagement

Evaluating youth civic engagement is not simple. As with many types of programs, youth civic engagement is complex, and "cannot be achieved by following a simple recipe" (Campbell-Patton & Patton, 2010, p. 601). For example, youth civic engagement can be evaluated at several levels and by consequences on individual(s), group(s), and community(ies). Most youth civic engagement program evaluations focus on individuals: "civic knowledge and activities of adolescents and youth and their attitudes toward and their actual later activities, such as participating civically, voting, and volunteering" (Higgins-D'Alessandro, 2010, p. 559). Most such evaluation remains focused on programmatic exposure and individual change and their links to later civic and political behavior. Higgins-D'Alessandro (2010) provided a comprehensive review of evaluation and research findings on the link between youth civic engagement programs and individual changes. Indeed, **civic engagement indicators** have been developed and are recommended to be used when evaluating youth civic engagement programs (Keeter, Zukin, Andolina, & Jenkins, 2002). These programmatic indicators and individual measures do not capture what is not seen—the political and civic meanings young people assign to (what adults might understand to be) everyday activities (VeLure Roholt, Hildreth, & Baizerman, 2008). Using the individual as the **unit of analysis** also fails to consider a primary characteristic of civic engagement work; it typically occurs in small youth groups. Youth civic engagement evaluations must also focus on group-level outcomes.

Using groups as the unit of analysis, evaluations describe and learn about changes in group membership, group leadership, interaction within the group, social networks developed within and outside of the group, and how groups of young people influence and have impact on local practices, programs, services, and policies. Here focus is less on changes in individual knowledge, skill, and attitude, and more on how well group members work together to address a public issue they find personally and collectively meaningful. Common evaluation questions are: Do they learn how to make a difference in this context? What have they learned about team work? How are the roles and tasks distributed throughout the group? How does the group accomplish what an individual member cannot do as easily or as well?

Emphasized is how each group member contributes to the group's work, highlighting how individuals do not know or need to know everything the group must know, or have skill in all relevant areas; individuals in and as a group can contribute meaningfully to their schools, youth organizations, and communities in ways difficult for individuals acting alone or as a nongroup collective. The knowledge and skills of the group are an important evaluation focus. Unlike evaluating on an individual level, group-level evaluations take all of this into consideration, examining what the group as a group does and how individuals contribute to the group. Evaluation can focus on and/or assess group knowledge, skill, and accomplishment, rather than on those of individual members. Evaluations of civic engagement can also focus on community-level outcomes.

Finally, youth civic engagement can also be evaluated on the community level and in at least two ways: the impact on the community's social capital and/or the impact on participatory structures and supports for young people. Winter (2003) provided insight on how youth civic engagement programs can be evaluated by examining the connections built within a community, and whether and how these work to support community social capital. One example of community-level evaluation is to study how the youth civic engagement initiative addresses declining social capital, because this is seen as essential for long-term, democratic vibrancy and health (Putnam, 2000). Other evaluators have studied the ways in which youth civic engagement programs create (or not) participatory structures for young people. Why this? Because "young people can surmount great odds and make significant contributions, but it is not reasonable to expect them to become civically engaged in communities and societies that fail to support them" (Yates & Youniss, 1999, p. 273). Here, the evaluation focus shifts from the individual and group, and to the impact of youth civic engagement programs on how communities are organized and how communities and civic groups work to invite and to support young people's contributions to local, civic affairs. These, too, can be part of an evaluation of youth civic engagement—the community and the local to national institutional arrangement and practices providing opportunity structures.

Our preference is not to evaluate individual development alone. A focus on individual development seems misplaced, when the program model focus is on collective civic and political activity—work typically done with others and focused on public concerns and issues. A focus on individual-level outcomes too easily ignores the social and political structural conditions (Yates & Youniss, 1999) that shape young people's civic and political involvement. An aphorism in evaluation studies illuminates the importance of attending to evaluation focus: "do we simply value what can be measured easily, or do we want to measure what we truly value?" This becomes a central question when considering how to design, implement, and use evaluation studies for civic youth work practice.

Evaluating Civic Youth Work: The Initiative

Civic youth work has most often been evaluated based on the youth development and learning outcomes (e.g., Checkoway & Richards-Schuster, 2003; Higgins-D'Alessandro, 2010; Sabo Flores, 2008). While important, this is not always what participants in civic youth work most value. Rather, it is easier to measure than other **outcomes**, and this may be why it is done. Young people in conversation do not emphasize what they have learned or how they have developed. What they did and how they together did it are what is important, more important to them than whether or not their project succeeded. Did they make a difference to the public issue they worked on? Did their work have any influence on others? If so, how?

Often, evaluations of youth civic engagement are not done democratically. This means that the participants are not involved in the design, planning, or data analysis (House & Howe, 2000). Consider this from another context (Chapter Five): Learning comes in part from doing correctly. Doing an evaluation democratically can teach democratic citizenship (Mathison, 2000). To evaluate a democratic practice, it is appropriate to use participatory (Cousins & Earl, 1995; Sabo Flores, 2008), responsive (Greene & Abma, 2001), and democratic (Ryan & DeStefano, 2000) evaluation methodological approaches and strategies. These normative, professional evaluation strategies support gathering useful, reliable, and valid data on program outcomes, to get at program effectiveness—did it work? These methodological approaches include inviting young people and others involved in the initiative to participate in the design, implementation, and use of the evaluation.

Evaluating Civic Youth Work: The Practice

There is relatively little on evaluation of practice, except studies of teachers (Cousins & Earl, 1995), and within some other caring professions (e.g., social work). The authors' evaluations done for Public Achievement in the U.S. and in Northern Ireland found that (civic) youth work skills was a significant contributor to or deflection from group practices and group achievement. Important evaluation questions here are:

1. What did the civic youth worker contribute to the groups' mastery of civic practice?
2. What did civic youth work contribute to the groups' involvement?
3. How do the young people describe their experience in the group?

An important distinction in practical evaluation is between process evaluation and outcome evaluation. The latter gets at final results, while the former is an early study of whether the program idea was implemented as conceived, and with what modification, i.e., the "fidelity" of putting the conception into practice. Process evaluation precedes outcome evaluation, because logically and practically, the evaluator must know what work is actually being done, how it is named and understood, and by whom, using what vocabulary. These must be known simply because this is the reality of what is to be evaluated. In effect, a process evaluation studies whether there is space or distortion between idea and programmatic reality, while outcome evaluation examines whether the program worked (for whom). This distinction is important, especially given the discussion in the previous chapter on civic youth work expertise. One first has to know if the civic youth worker is at least competent to know if civic youth work has actually been implemented at this site, with these young people. Otherwise, the evaluation is simply a youth work evaluation and not a civic youth work evaluation. Also important is a clear understanding of the logic of civic youth work, presented next.

Two tools in vogue for designing evaluation studies are the related Program Model and **Evaluation Logic Model**. The first presents the theories and practices which are thought and used to bring about youth civic engagement, while the second is the program (practice) model presented as a frame for a valid, practical, usable, high-quality evaluation of civic youth work. The civic youth work logic model in Table 6.2 shows the relationship between the different civic youth work descriptions presented in this primer. Shown is how civic youth work can be evaluated at the individual, group, and community levels.

The inputs are what are needed to start civic youth work. In civic youth work, these are relatively basic, and include a civic youth worker, a small group of young people, and any materials that are needed to work on their issue. The activities are the ten steps described in Chapter Four. When these are joined to the touchstones from Chapter Five, the outputs of civic youth work practice emerge. When these are done, civic youth work supports outcomes for young people (individuals), the group, and the community. This is presented in Table 6.2.

Table 6.2. Civic Youth Work Practice Logic Model

Inputs	Activities	Outputs	Outcomes
1. Civic youth worker. 2. Young people. 3. Materials as needed to work on issue.	1. "Something needs to change." 2. "Let's do something about it, together." 3. Understanding what needs to change. 4. Deciding what to do. 5. Figuring out how to do it and rehearsing. 6. Doing it! 7. Celebrating, reflecting on, evaluating, and improving on what was done. 8. What to do next? 9. Working on the issue. 10. Spreading the word.	1. Group is formed. 2. Group meets regularly. 3. Issue/topic is chosen. 4. Issue/topic is researched. 5. Plan is developed to address issue. 6. Actions group decided on are rehearsed in small group. 7. Group takes public action on issue/topic. 8. Group celebrates what they have done. 9. Group evaluates what they did and if it made a difference. 10. Group decides what they want to do next. 11. If chosen, work on same issue continues, or work on a new topic/issue begins.	Individual: • Beginning mastery of group civic practice and citizen role. • Experience self as citizen. • Enhanced likelihood of lifelong civic engagement. Group: • Group becomes "group" to members. • Group functions democratically. • Group learns what to do to take action on public issues. Community: • People know about group's issue. • Change occurs on group's issue. • Similar work by young people is supported in more places throughout the community.

We can envision how this simple civic youth work logic model can be expanded and enriched by creating questions from the research literature reviewed in the primer and placing them into this logic model to show what an evaluation of a research-based practice could look like. Another way to deepen and enrich the model is to consider the place of young people in evaluating civic youth work.

The Places of Youth in Evaluation

There are many reasons to invite young people to be cocreators of youth civic engagement and civic youth work initiatives evaluation designs, including those they are involved in. Their involvement in evaluation supports their learning and development in complementary and even identical civic youth work domains, including: social competencies, self-confidence, civic competencies, social capital, and identity exploration (Sabo Flores, 2008). "Youth participatory evaluation" is an evaluation practice which simultaneously supports citizen and youth development, while contributing to the collection of good data on what they did, how they did it, and how all of this matters to them, to others, and to their community (Sabo Flores, 2008; VeLure Roholt, Hildreth, & Baizerman, 2008). Doing evaluations in this way supports their work on their public issue. Youth civic engagement projects "often succeed when young people learn how to evaluate their own actions and use this learning in their ongoing project work" (VeLure Roholt, Hildreth, & Baizerman, 2008, p. 79). **Youth participatory evaluation** is a form of civic youth work, when done within a civic youth work frame (VeLure Roholt, Baizerman, & Hildreth, 2013).

Youth participation in community research and evaluation has quickly become a recognized field of practice with a core set of principles to guide practice and a working definition:

> Youth participation in community evaluation research involves young people in knowledge development at the community level. The process includes efforts by adults to involve young people in the research or evaluation of public agencies and private institutions; by young people to organize their own research or evaluation projects; and by youth and adults to work together in intergenerational relationships. (Checkoway, Dobbie, & Richards-Schuster, 2003)

Youth participatory evaluation is a "democratic process" that works to equalize power relationships between young people and adults (Checkoway, Dobbie, et al., 2003), as does civic youth work practice.

Involving young people as coevaluators addresses concerns raised by child rights scholars (Percy-Smith, 2010), that young people are often consulted, but rarely do their ideas influence program, practice, or policy. Percy-Smith (2010) argued that this is frequently because youth participation often remains focused on consultation rather than on creating an "active process of involvement in learning and change" (p. 110). When adhering to the outlined principles (Checkoway, Dobbie, et al., 2003), young people can become active and valuable partners in describing and learning from youth civic engagement efforts. In our own evaluations of youth civic engagement programs, young people taught us how everyday activities could be read and experienced as political. For us, the youth were making a telephone call to gather information. To them, this action required courage, and further reinforced the idea that they could gather necessary information to move their public project. Without their involvement, their naming of their work and experience, it is easy to miss the value of the practice and the larger initiatives. This shows that we do not see, experience, or interpret actions and behaviors the same way. For an evaluator these are crucial data.

Youth-Enhancing Evaluation Strategies

There is now a rich literature and practice history of youth participatory or youth-led evaluation work (Checkoway & Richards-Schuster, 2003; London, 2000; Sabo, 2003; Sabo Flores, 2008; Shumer, 2007, 2013). This work provides perspectives and conceptualizations that support youth participatory evaluation studies, and that offer tools and techniques to introduce evaluation to young people (and others), train them in evaluation methods, and facilitate the completion of a high-quality evaluation study. These methods support the democratic evaluation requirements of inclusion, dialogue, and deliberation (House & Howe, 2000).

Inviting young people's involvement in evaluating their own and other youth civic engagement efforts addresses this inclusion requirement of democratic evaluation. Inclusion means "that all those who have legitimate, relevant interests should be included in decisions that affect those interests" (House & Howe, 2000, p. 5). Youth participatory evaluation supports inclusion by working with young people so they can formulate their ideas for the evaluation and advocate for this. Many youth involvement projects often fail at creating appropriate ways to support young people giving good advice. Often, adult processes and structures are used, and young people are often blamed for not contributing when participating in these (Percy-Smith, 2010). Youth participatory evaluation can deal with this concern. There are many creative methods, such as photo voice (McIntyre, 2000), and alternative frameworks to guide an evaluation. One is theater (Sabo Flores, 2008). Others, too (Checkoway & Richards-Schuster, 2003), have been used successfully to support young people's involvement in an evaluation study. It is critical to not expect that young people will know how to express their opinions in adult-like ways and in adult-like structures. Building a space where young people can have their own voice and speak it their own ways also supports the second requirement of democratic evaluation, dialogue.

Much of the writing on youth participation (Checkoway & Richards-Schuster, 2003; Hart, 1992) has focused either explicitly or implicitly on how **dialogue** can be nurtured among adults and young people, or among young people within a group. House and Howe's (2000) description of dialogue as a requirement for democratic evaluation can be heard in the definition provided by Burbules (1993):

> Although it is possible to consider any sort of conversation as dialogue, here I want to limit the term to refer to a particular kind of pedagogical communicative relation: a conversational interaction directed intentionally towards teaching and learning. (p. x)

Obvious and often missing from these conversations is that dialogue is a space, ethos, and skill, and that these take time to nurture and require endurance to sustain, as practitioners as well as the scholars of dialogical philosophy and theory know (e.g., Buber, 1958; Burbules, 1993; Wells, 1999). To invite and support young people's participation in evaluation studies, it is essential that the work be thought of as long-term and ongoing. It is unrealistic to expect young people to participate successfully and helpfully in an evaluation study of their own or other youth's work when they are not invited in early to the evaluation process, and when dialogue between them and the evaluator is not regular, ongoing, substantive, and used. True dialogue supports deliberation, the final requirement of democratic evaluation.

As a requirement of democratic evaluation, deliberation makes explicit the values basic to the work. "Evaluation is a procedure for determining values, which are emergent and transformed through deliberative processes" (House & Howe, 2000, p. 8). As a process, deliberation supports ongoing and thoughtful conversations and considerations of what is going on, what is the meaning of what one is doing, does it matter, and to whom?

Given this, deliberation provides both focus and method to youth participatory evaluations. Activities and conversations should focus on clarifying values, as well as on describing a program; indeed, the program or practice may not be fully described until we can understand the value-base of the work as *experienced by par-*

ticipants. Deliberation also supports methods that pose questions for youth group members to consider, respond to, and/or take a stand on. In the process, values are often disclosed.

Taken together, these three ethical-methodological groundings for youth participatory evaluation show that it is possible, surely helpful, and likely most useful to include young people in evaluation in ways meaningful, real, and consequential to them, to the evaluator, to the study, and to others. We next weave together the several strands covered in this chapter.

Conclusions

Evaluation can be useful, and may be required, for practice mastery and improvement. In evaluating civic youth work practice, recommended are participatory and democratic approaches and methods. These complement the practice and further support the creation of a vibrant, democratic space. We offered here a practice logic model, based on the overall description of practice presented throughout this primer. This model provides one way of conceptualizing how doing civic youth work is connected to being a civic youth worker, and how both of these support particular outcomes for young people, the group, and the larger community. We recommend that the evaluation be designed to further support this democratic practice with young people.

Including young people in the design and implementation of the evaluation study is recommended, as this supports again the overall civic youth work philosophy, ethos, and craft orientation, and fits with participating young people's experiences and expectations. It also is likely to lead to strong and trustworthy data, which capture the full range of civic youth work practice outcomes, both what is visible and what is meaningful for both the civic youth worker and young people.

Reflective Questions

1. What is the value of doing a "process evaluation" of a new or existing civic youth work project?
2. To you, is evaluation a science, in the sense that physics is?
3. How do you distinguish evaluation from assessment and monitoring, and from formal social science or behavioral science research?

4. Where in a report of an evaluation study do you find "the best stuff" for use in policy-making, program improvement, or decision-making?
5. Can an evaluation study done six years ago in Uganda on a youth civic engagement program be useful to you?

Glossary

Civic engagement indicators: These are developed based on research evidence to guide civic engagement programs in design and practice to support long-term civic engagement. Examples include working to solve community problems, regular voting, and participating in a fund-raiser.

Dialogue: A form of communication that has been advocated by many including Paulo Freire, the critical educator and scholar; and Martin Buber, a famous Jewish theologian. This form of communication emphasizes addressing power imbalances and equalizing power in communication so that everyone has equal opportunity to participate in the conversation and discussion. Through dialogue, participants seek not only to hear what the other person(s) has (have) to say, but also to learn more about who they are, and to understand what are their central concerns.

Evaluation Logic Model: As described by Wyatt Knowlton & Phillips (2013), a logic model is "a visual method of presenting an idea. It offers a way to describe and share an understanding of relationships (or connections) among elements necessary to operate a program or change effort (p. 4)."

Outcomes: These refer to the intended results of a program or practice. It is the changes or the state of affairs that the effort sought to bring about, and if successful, has created.

Participatory evaluation: A normative, professional evaluation approach that emphasizes stakeholder involvement in designing and implementing an evaluation study, including: developing an evaluation focus and questions, gathering and collecting data from different sources, analyzing the data, and reporting on what was learned. This approach has been linked to better utilization of evaluation findings.

Unit of analysis: The major entity being studies; often referred to as the what or whom that the study is focusing on.

Youth participatory evaluation: A cousin of participatory evaluation that has gained recognition in the last ten years. This increasingly normative, professional evaluation methodology partners with young people to evaluate programs, often ones they are participating in. The methodology aims to complete a competent and high-quality evaluation study, and to support young people's civic, critical-thinking, social, and personal development. It has also worked to challenge typical age-roles and views of young people as deficient and incompetent.

Bibliography

African News Service. (2003). Youth participation is imperative for building a better world, says Commonwealth Secretary-General. *African News Service*, May 28, p. 1008148u8143.

Aitken, S. (2001). *Geographies of young people: The morally contested spaces of identity.* London, UK: Routledge.

Aitken, S., Lund, R., & Kjorholt, A. (Eds.). (2008). *Global childhoods: Globalization, development, and young people.* New York, NY: Routledge.

Amna, E., & Zetterberg, P. (2010). A political science perspective on socialization research: Young Nordic citizens in a comparative light. In L. Sherrod, J. Torney-Purta, & C. A. Flanagan (Eds.), *Handbook of research on civic engagement in youth* (pp. 43–66). Hoboken, NJ: John Wiley.

Andolina, W., Jenkins, K., Zukin, C., & Keeter, S. (2003). Habits from home, lessons from school: Influences on youth civic engagement. *Social Education, 67*(6), 333–338.

Ansell, N. (2005). *Children, youth and development.* London, UK: Routledge.

Appadurai, A. (2006). The right to research. *Globalisation, Societies and Education, 4*(2), 167–177.

Argyris, C. (1993). *Knowledge for action: A guide to overcoming barriers to organizational change.* San Francisco, CA: Jossey-Bass.

Arnett, R., & Arneson, P. (1999). *Dialogic civility in a cynical age: Community, hope, and interpersonal relationships.* Albany, NY: State University of New York Press.

Aronson, R. (2012, November 30). Place your bets: Sartre and the underdog. *The Times Literary Supplement*, p. 17. Retrieved from http://www.is.wayne.edu/raronson/Articles/TLS%20Nov%2712.pdf

Baizerman, M. (1974). Towards analysis of the relations among youth counterculture, telephone hotlines, and anonymity. *Journal of Youth and Adolescence, 3*(4), 293–306.

Baizerman, M. (1976). *Self-evaluation handbook for hotlines and youth crisis centers.* Minneapolis, MN: Center for Youth Development and Research, University of Minnesota.

Baizerman, M. (1995). Why does a community need its adolescents? *Community Education Journal, 22*(3–4), 29–31.

Baizerman, M. (1998). It's only 'human nature': Revisiting the denaturalization of adolescence. *Child & Youth Care Forum, 28*(6), 437–444.

Ballet, J., Biggeri, M., & Comim, F. (2011). Children's agency and the capability approach: A conceptual framework. In M. Biggeri, J. Ballet, & F. Comim (Eds.), *Children and the capability approach* (pp. 22–45). Hampshire, UK: Palgrave Macmillan.

Banks, J. (1997). *Educating citizens in a multicultural society.* New York, NY: Teachers College Press.

Banks, J. (2001). Citizenship education and diversity: Implications for teacher education. *Journal of Teacher Education, 52*(1), 5–16.

Barrett, W. (1979). *The illusion of technique: A search for meaning in a technological civilization.* New York, NY: Anchor Press.

Bass, M. (1997). Citizenship and young people's role in public life. *National Civic Review, 86*(3), 203–211.

Battistoni, R. (2000). Service learning and civic education. In S. Mann & J. Patrick (Eds.), *Education for civic engagement in democracy: Service learning and other promising practices* (pp. 29–44). Bloomington, IN: ERIC Clearinghouse for Social Studies/Social Science Education.

Belton, B. (2009). *Developing critical youth work theory: Building professional judgment in the community context.* Rotterdam, The Netherlands: Sense.

Benner, P. (1994). *Interpretive phenomenology: Embodiment, caring, and the ethics in health and illness.* Thousand Oaks, CA: Sage.

Bennett, A. (2000). *Popular music and youth culture: Music, identity and place.* New York, NY: Palgrave Macmillan.

Bennett, S. (2000). Political apathy and avoidance of news media among generation X and Y: America's continuing problem. In S. Mann & J. Patrick (Eds.), *Education for civic engagement in democracy: Service learning and other promising practices* (pp. 9–28). Bloomington, IN: ERIC Clearinghouse for Social Studies/Social Science Education.

Bennett, S. (1997). Why young Americans hate politics, and what we should do about it. *PS, 30*(1), 47–52.

Bensman, J., & Lilienfeld, R. (1973). *Craft and consciousness: Occupational technique and the development of world images.* New York, NY: Wiley.

Berman, S. (1997). *Children's social consciousness and the development of social responsibility.* Albany, NY: State University of New York Press.

Biggeri, M., Ballet, J., & Comim, F. (Eds.). (2011). *Children and the capability approach.* Hampshire, UK: Palgrave Macmillan.

Billig, S. (2000). The effects of service learning. *The School Administrator, 57*(7), 14–18.

Boal, A. (1979). *Theater of the oppressed.* New York, NY: Urizen Books.

Boud, D., Cohen, R., & Walker, D. (Eds.). (1993). *Using experience for learning.* Buckingham, UK: Open University Press.

Boud, D., & Miller, N. (1996). *Working with experience: Animating learning.* New York, NY: Routledge.

Boyte, H. (1991). Community service and civic education. *Phi Delta Kappan, 72*(10), 765–767.

Boyte, H., & Farr, J. (1997). The work of citizenship and the problem of service-learning. In R. Battistoni & W. Hudson (Eds.), *Experiencing citizenship: Concepts and models for service-learning in political science* (pp. 35–48). Washington, DC: American Association for Higher Education.

Boyte, H C., and Kari, N. (1996) Democracy of the people: Expanding citizen capacity in *Capacity for Change? The Nonprofit World in the Age of Devolution* (pp. 109–124). Indianapolis IN:University Center on Philanthropy, 1996.

Boyte, H. C., & Skelton, N. (1997). The legacy of public work: Educating for citizenship. *Educational Leadership, 54*(5), 12–17.

Buber, M. (1958). *I and thou.* New York, NY: Scribner.

Burbules, N. C. (1993). *Dialogue in teaching: Theory and practice.* New York, NY: Teachers College Press.

Burfoot, D. (2003). Arguing for a better future: Children and young people's participation. *Youth Studies Australia, 22*(3), 44–52.

Butts, R. F. (1980). *The revival of civic learning: A rationale for citizenship education in American schools.* Bloomington, IN: Phi Delta Kappa Educational Foundation.

Byrne Fields, A. (n.d.). *The youth challenge: Participating in democracy.* New York, NY: Carnegie Corporation of New York.

Camino, L. (2000). Youth adult partnerships: Entering new territory in community work and research. *Applied Developmental Science, 4*(S1), 11–20.

Cammarota, J., & Fine, M. (2008). *Revolutionizing education: Youth participatory action research in motion.* New York, NY: Routledge.

Campbell, N. (Ed.), (2000). *The radiant hour: Versions of youth in American culture.* Exeter, UK: University of Exeter Press.

Campbell-Patton, C., & Patton, M. Q. (2010). Conceptualizing and evaluating the complexities of youth civic engagement. In L. Sherrod, J. Torney-Purta, & C. A. Flanagan (Eds.), *Handbook of research on civic engagement in youth* (pp. 593–619). Hoboken, NJ: John Wiley.

Carse, J. (1987). *Finite and infinite games.* New York, NY: Free Press.

Center for Democracy and Citizenship. (2001). *Our philosophy*. Retrieved from http://www.publicwork.org/1_2_philosophy.html

Chawla, L. (2002). *Growing up in an urbanising world*. London, UK: UNESCO.

Checkoway, B., Dobbie, D., & Richards-Schuster, K. (2003). Involving young people in community evaluation research. *Community Youth Development Journal, 4*(1), 7–11.

Checkoway, B., & Gutierrez, L. (2006). Youth participation and community change: An introduction. *Journal of Community Practice, 14*(1–2), 1–9.

Checkoway, B., & Richards-Schuster, K. (2003). Youth participation in community evaluation research. *American Journal of Evaluation, 24*(1), 21–33.

Checkoway, B., Richards-Schuster, K., Abdullah, S., Aragon, M., Facio, E., Figueroa, L., Reddy, E., & White, A. (2003). Young people as competent citizens. *Community Development Journal: An International Forum, 38*(4), 298–309.

Chilcoat, G., & Ligon, J. (1998a). Theatre as an emancipatory tool: Classroom drama in the Mississippi Freedom Schools. *Journal of Curriculum Studies, 30*(5), 515–543.

Chilcoat, G., & Ligon, J. (1998b). 'We talk here. This is a school for talking.' Participatory democracy from the classroom out into the community: How discussion was used in the Mississippi Freedom Schools. *Curriculum Inquiry, 28*(2), 165–193.

Chilcoat, G., & Ligon, J. (2001). Discussion as a means for transformative change: Social studies lessons from the Mississippi Freedom Schools. *Social Studies, 92*(5), 213–219.

Child Protection Working Group. (2012). *Minimum standards for child protection in humanitarianaction*. Retrieved from http://cpwg.net/wpcontent/uploads/2012/10/Minimum-standards-for-child-protection-in-humanitarian-action.pdf

Chilisa, B. (2012). *Indigenous research methodologies*. Thousand Oaks, CA: Sage.

Christian, C. (2003). Youth work education and training: From training to professional education. *Commonwealth Youth and Development, 1*(2), 69–86.

CIRCLE (2003). *The civic mission of schools*. College Park, MD: University of Maryland.

CIRCLE (n.d.). *Civic engagement indicators*. Retrieved from http://www.civicyouth.org/practitioners/Core_Indicators_Page.htm

Cohen, M. Z., Kahn, D. L., & Steeves, R. H. (2000). *Hermeneutic phenomenological research: A practical guide for nurse researchers*. Thousand Oaks, CA: Sage.

Coles, R. (1986). *The political life of children*. New York, NY: Atlantic Monthly Press.

Comber, M. (2003, November). *Civic curriculum and civic skills: Recent evidence*. Retrieved from http://www.civicyouth.org/research/products/fact_sheets.htm (no longer accessible).

Comim, F., Ballet, J., Biggeri, M., & Iervese, V. (2011). Introduction. In M. Biggeri, J. Ballet, & F. Comim (Eds.), *Children and the capability approach* (pp. 3–21). Hampshire, UK: Palgrave Macmillan.

Cone, R. (2003). Service-learning and civic education: Challenging assumptions. *Peer Review, 5*(3), 12–15.

Corsaro, W. (1997). *The sociology of childhood*. Thousand Oaks, CA: Pine Forge Press.

Crain, W. (1985). *Theories of development*. Indianapolis, IN: Prentice Hall.

Cousins, J. B., & Earl, L. (Eds.). (1995). *Participatory evaluation in education: Studies in evaluation use and organizational learning*. New York, NY: Falmer Press.

Dahl, R. (1998). *On democracy*. New Haven, CT: Yale University Press.

Dalrymple, J. (2006). Constructions of the child and youth advocacy: Emerging issues in advocacy practice. *Child and Society, 19*(1), 3–15.

Danesi, M. (2003). *My son is an alien: A cultural portrait of today's youth*. Lanham, MD: Rowman & Littlefield.

Davis I., Gregory, I., & Riley, S. (1999). *Good citizenship and educational provision*. London, UK: Falmer Press.

Delgado, M. (2002). *New frontiers for youth development in the twenty-first century: Revitalizing and broadening youth development*. New York, NY: Columbia University Press.

Delgado, M., & Staples, L. (2008). *Youth-led community organizing: Theory and action*. Oxford, UK: Oxford University Press.

Delli Carpini, M., & Keeter, S. (1996). *What Americans know about politics and why it matters*. New Haven, CT: Yale University Press.

———. (2000). What should be learned through service learning? *PS, 33*(3), 635–637.

de Tocqueville, A. (1966). *Democracy in America* (G. Lawrence, Trans.). New York, NY: Harper.

Dewey, J. (1916). *Democracy and education*. New York, NY: Free Press.

Dewey, J. (1927). *The public and its problems*. Athens, OH: Swallow Press.

Dynneson, T. L., & Gross, R. E. (1991). The educational perspective: Citizenship education in American society. In R. E. Gross & T. L. Dynneson (Eds.), *Social science perspectives on citizenship education* (pp. 1–42). New York, NY: Teachers College Press.

Dreyfus, H. (2001). *On the internet*. New York, NY: Routledge.

Dreyfus, H., & Dreyfus, S. (1991). Towards a phenomenology of ethical expertise. *Human Studies, 14*(4), 229–250.

Dreyfus, H., & Dreyfus, S. (2004). The ethical implications of the five-stage skill-acquisition model. *Bulletin of Science Technology and Society, 24*(3), 251–264.

Driskell, D. (2002). *Creating better cities with children and youth: A manual for participation*. London, UK: Earthscan.

Duffy, M. (2000). Schools can't compensate for society. *New Statesman, 129*(4517), 23–24.

Duncan-Andrade, J., & Morrell, E. (2008). *The art of critical pedagogy: Possibilities for moving from theory to practice in urban schools*. New York, NY: Peter Lang.

Dworkin, J. B., Larson, R., & Hansen, D. (2003). Adolescents' accounts of growth experiences in youth activities. *Journal of Youth and Adolescence, 32*(1), 17–26.

Eccles, J., Barber, B., Stone, M., & Hunt, J. (2003). Extracurricular activities and adolescent development. *Journal of Social Issues, 59*(4), 865–890.

Eliasoph, N. (1998). *Avoiding politics: How Americans produce apathy in everyday life*. Cambridge, UK: Cambridge University Press.

Emery, K., Braselmann, S., & Reid, L.R. (2004). Introduction: Freedom summer and Freedom Schools. Retrieved from: http://www.educationanddemocracy.org/FSCfiles/A_02_introduction.htm

Epstein, J. (1998). *Youth culture: Identity in a postmodern world*. Oxford, UK: Blackwell.

Ericsson, A. (2006). *The Cambridge handbook of expertise and expert performance*. New York, NY: Cambridge University Press.

Evans, S. M., & Boyte, H. C. (1986). *Free spaces: The sources of democratic change in America*. New York, NY: Harper & Row.

Eyler, J., & Giles, D. (1999). *Where's the learning in service-learning?* San Francisco, CA: Jossey-Bass.

Farquhar, E. C., & Dawson, K. S. (1979). *Citizen education today—Developing civil competencies*. Washington, DC: Department of Health, Education, and Welfare; U.S. Office of Education.

Finn, J. L., & Checkoway, B. (1998). Young people as competent community builders: A challenge to social work. *Social Work, 43*(4), 335–345.

Foley, G. (1999). *Learning in social action: A contribution to understanding informal education*. London, UK: Zed Books.

Foran, A., & Olson, M. (2008). Seeking pedagogical places. *Phenomenology & Practice, 2*(1), 24–48.

Forner, A. (1974). Age stratification and age conflict in political life. *American Sociological Review, 39*(2), 187–196.

Fowler, D. (1990). Democracy's next generation. *Educational Leadership, 48*(3), 10–15.

Freire, P. (1970). *Pedagogy of the oppressed*. New York, NY: Continuum.

Friedman, M. (1972). *Touchstones of reality: Existential trust and the community of peace*. New York, NY: E. P. Dutton.

Friedman, M. (1988). Dialogue, confirmation, and the image of the human. *Journal of Humanistic Psychology, 28*(2), 123–135.

Frønes, I. (1994). Dimensions of childhood. In J. Qvortrup, M. Bardy, G. Sgritta, & H. Wintersberger (Eds.), *Childhood matters: Social theory, practice, and politics*. Aldershot, UK: Avebury.

Gadamer, H. (1985). *Truth and method*. New York, NY: The Crossroads Publishing Company.

Gallup, G., & Gallup, A. (2000). American teens need a history lesson. Retrieved from http://www.gallup.com/poll/2935/American-Teens-Need-History-Lesson.aspx

Gibson, C. (2001). *From inspiration to participation: A review of perspectives on youth civic engagement*. New York, NY: Carnegie Corporation of New York.

Gimpel, J., Lay, J. C., & Schuknecht, J. (2003). *Cultivating democracy: Civic environments and political socialization in America*. Washington, DC: Brookings Institution Press.

Ginwright, S. (2010). *Black youth rising: Activism and radical healing in urban America*. New York, NY: Teachers College Press.

Ginwright, S., & Cammarota, J. (2002). New terrain in youth development: The promise of a social justice approach. *Social Justice, 29*(4), 82–95.

Ginwright, S., & Cammarota, J., & Noguera, P. (2005). Youth, social justice, and communities: Toward a theory of urban youth policy. *Social Justice, 32*(3), 24–40.

Ginwright, S., Noguera, P., & Cammarota, J. (2006). *Beyond resistance: Youth activism and community change: New democratic possibilities for practice and policy for America's youth.* New York, NY: Routledge.

Giroux, H. A. (2010, October 17). Lessons from Paulo Freire. *The Chronicle of Higher Education.* Retrieved from http://chronicle.com/article/Lessons-From-Paulo-Freire/124910/

Gitlin, A., & Smyth, J. (1989). *Teacher evaluation: Educative alternatives.* New York, NY: Falmer Press.

Goncu, A. (1999). *Children's engagement in the world: Sociocultural perspectives.* Cambridge, UK: Cambridge University Press.

Goranzon, B., Hammaren, M., & Ennals, J. R. (2006). *Dialogue, skill and tacit knowledge.* Chichester, UK: J. Wiley.

Gordan, H. (2010). *We fight to win: Inequality and the politics of youth activism.* New Brunswick, NJ: Rutgers University Press.

Gorham, E. (1992). *National service, citizenship, and political education.* Albany, NY: State University of New York Press.

Greene, J. C., & Abma, T. A. (2001). *Responsive evaluation.* San Francisco, CA: Jossey-Bass.

Griffin, C. (1993). *Representations of youth: The study of youth and adolescence in Britain and America.* Cambridge, UK: Polity Press.

Gubrium, J. F., Holstein, J. A., & Buckholdt, D. R. (1994). *Constructing the life course.* Dix Hills, NY: General Hall.

Guy, A. (1991). The role of Aristotle's praxis today. *Journal of Value Inquiry, 25*(3), 287–289.

Hahn, C. (1998). Becoming political: Comparative perspectives on citizenship education. Albany, NY: State University of New York Press.

Hall, J., Ahn, J., & Greene, J. (2012). Values engagement in evaluation: Ideas, illustrations, and implications. *American Journal of Evaluation, 33*(2), 195–207.

Hart, R. (1992). *Children's participation: From tokenism to citizenship.* Florence, Italy: UNICEF International Child Development Centre.

Hart, R. (1999). *Children's participation: The theory and practice of involving young citizens in community development and environmental care.* London, NY: Earthscan.

Haste, H. (2010). Citizenship education: A critical look at a contested field. In L. Sherrod, J. Torney-Purta, & C. A. Flanagan (Eds.), *Handbook of research on civic engagement in youth* (pp. 161–188). Hoboken, NJ: John Wiley.

Hekman, S. J. (1983). *Weber, the ideal type, and contemporary social theory.* Notre Dame, IN: University of Notre Dame Press.

Hepburn, M., Niemi, R., & Chapman, C. (2000). Service learning in college political science: Queries and commentary. *PS, 33*(3), 617–622.

Higgins-D'Alessandro, A. (2010). The transdisciplinary nature of citizenship and civic/political engagement evaluaton. In L. Sherrod, J. Torney-Purta, & C. A. Flanagan (Eds.), *Handbook of research on civic engagement in youth* (pp. 559–592). Hoboken, NJ: John Wiley.

Higgs, J., Titchen, A., & Neville, V. (2001). Professional practice and knowledge. In J. Higgs & A. Titchen (Eds.), *Practice knowledge and expertise in the health professions* (pp. 3–9). Oxford, UK: Butterworth-Heinemann.

Hildreth, R. (1998). *Building worlds, transforming lives, making history: A guide to public achievement.* Minneapolis, MN: Center for Democracy and Citizenship.

Hildreth, R.W. & VeLure Roholt, R. (2013). Teaching and training civic youth workers: Creating spaces for reciprocal civic and youth development. In R. VeLure Roholt, M. Baizerman, & R.W. Hildreth (Eds.) *Civic youth work: Cocreating democratic youth spaces* (pp. 151–159). Chicago, IL: Lyceum Press.

Hirsch, E. D. (1997). Why traditional education is more progressive? *The American Enterprise, 8*(2), 42–46.

Hirsch, E. D. (1999). Americanization and the schools. *The Clearing House, 72*(3), 136–140.

Hockey, J., & James, A. (1993). *Growing up and growing old: Ageing and dependency in the life course.* London, UK: Sage.

Hockey, J., & James, A. (2003). *Social identities across the life course.* New York, NY: Palgrave Macmillan.

Holden, C., & Clough, N. (1998). *Children as citizens: Education for participation.* London, UK: Jessica Kingsley.

Horton, M., & Freire, P. (1990). *We make the road by walking: Conversations on education and social change.* Philadelphia, PA: Temple University Press.

House, E., & Howe, K. (2000). Deliberative democratic evaluation. *New Directions for Evaluation, 85*, 3–12.

Hunter, S., & Brisbin, R. (2000). The impact of service learning on democratic and civic values. *PS, 33*(3), 623–626.

James, A. (2011). To be (come) or not to be (come): Understanding children's citizenship. *The Annals of the American Academy of Political and Social Science, 633*(1), 167–179.

James, A., Jenks, C., & Prout, A. (1998). *Theorizing childhood.* Cambridge, UK: Polity Press.

James, A., & Prout, A. (1997). *Constructing and reconstructing childhood* (2nd ed.). London, UK: Falmer Press.

Jeffs, T. (2001). Citizenship, youth work and democratic renewal. *Scottish Youth Issues Journal, 2*(1), 11–34.

Jenks, C. (1996). *Childhood.* London, UK: Routledge.

Jennings, M. K., Langton, K. P., & Niemi, R. G. (1974). Effects of the high school civics curriculum. In M. K. Jennings & R. G. Niemi (Eds.), *The political character of adolescence* (pp. 181–207). Princeton, NJ: Princeton University Press.

John, M. (2003). *Children's rights and power: Charging up for a new century*. London, UK: Jessica Kingsley.

Johnson, D., & Johnson, R. (1975). *Learning together and alone: Cooperation, competition, and individualization*. Englewood Cliffs, NJ: Prentice-Hall.

Keeter, S., Zukin, C., Andolina, M., & Jenkins, K. (2002). *The civic and political health of the nation: A generational portrait*. Center for Information and Research on Civic Learning and Engagement. Retrieved from http://www.civicyouth.org/research/products/Civic_Political_Health.pdf

Kennelly, J. (2009). Good citizen/bad activist: The cultural role of the state in youth activism. *The Review of Education, Pedagogy, and Cultural Studies, 31*(2–3), 127–149.

Kielsmeier, J. (2000, May). A time to serve, a time to learn: Service-learning and the promise of democracy. *Phi Delta Kappan, 81*(9), 652–657.

Kincheloe, J. (2008). *Critical pedagogy* (2nd ed.). New York, NY: Peter Lang.

Kirkpatrick, D. (2012, September 17). Cultural clash fuels Muslims raging at film. *The New York Times*, p. A1.

Kirshner, B. (2006). Apprenticeship learning in youth activism. In S. Ginwright, P. Noguera, & J. Cammarota (Eds.), *Beyond resistance: Youth activism and community change: New possibilities for practice and policy for America's youth* (pp. 37–58). New York, NY: Routledge.

Kirshner, B., O'Donoghue, J., & McLaughlin, M. (2002). *Youth participation: Improving institutions and communities*. San Francisco, CA: Jossey-Bass.

Klein, A. (1953). *Society, democracy and the group: An analysis of social objectives*. New York, NY: Women's Press and W. Morrow.

Koberg, D., & Bagnall, J. (1981). *The all new universal traveler: A soft-systems guide to creativity, problem-solving, and the process of reaching goals*. Los Altos, CA: W. Kaufmann.

Kolb, D. A. (1984). *Experiential learning: Experience as the source of learning and development*. Englewood Cliffs, NJ: Prentice-Hall.

Konopka, G. (1963). *Social group work: A helping process*. Englewood Cliffs, NJ: Prentice Hall.

Laing, R.D. (1970). *Knots*. New York, NY: Pantheon Books.

Lakoff, G., & Johnson, M. (2003). *Metaphors we live by* (2nd edition). Chicago, IL: University of Chicago Press.

Lansdown, G. (2005). *The evolving capacities of the child*. Florence, Italy: Innocenti Research Center.

Lave, J., & Wenger, E. (1991). *Situated learning: Legitimate peripheral participation*. Cambridge, UK: Cambridge University Press.

Lee, N. (2001). *Childhood and society*. Buckingham, UK: Open University Press.

Lemann, N. (1996). Kicking in groups. *The Atlantic Monthly, 277*(4), 22–25.

Lerner, R., & Steinberg, L. (2009). The scientific study of adolescent development: Historical and contemporary perspectives. In R. Lerner & L. Steinberg (Eds., 3rd ed.), *Handbook of adolescent psychology: Volume 1: Individual bases of adolescent development* (pp. 3–14). Hoboken, NJ: John Wiley.

Lesko, N. (2001). *Act your age! A cultural construction of adolescence.* New York, NY: RoutledgeFalmer.

Levinas, E. (1969). *Totality and infinity: An essay on exteriority.* (A. Lingis Trans.) Pittsburgh, PA: Duquesne University Press.

Levine, J. (2002). *Harmful to minors: The perils of protecting children from sex.* Minneapolis, MN: University of Minnesota Press.

Levinson, M. (2012). *No citizen left behind.* Cambridge, MA: Harvard University Press.

Lincoln, Y., & Guba, E.(1985). *Naturalistic inquiry.* Thousand Oaks, CA: Sage Publications.

Linds, W., Goulet, L., & Sammel, A. (Eds.). (2010). *Participatory practices: Adult/youth engagement for social and environmental justice.* Rotterdam, The Netherlands: Sense.

London, J. (2000). Youth-led research, evaluation, and planning: The experience of youth in focus. *Focal Point,* Summer, 34–35.

Magnuson, D., & Baizerman, M. (2007). *Work with youth in divided and contested societies.* Rotterdam, The Netherlands: Sense.

Malamud, R. (1998). *Reading zoos: Representations of animals and captivity.* New York, NY: New York University Press.

Males, M. (1996). *The scapegoat generation: America's war on adolescents.* Monroe, ME: Common Courage Press.

Mallan, K., & Pearce, S. (2003). *Youth cultures: Texts, images, and identities.* Westport, CT: Praeger.

Malone, K., & Hartung, C. (2010). Challenges of participatory practice with children. In B. Percy-Smith & N. Thomas (Eds.), *A handbook of children and young people's participation: Perspectives from theory and practice* (pp. 24–38). New York, NY: Routledge.

Mann, S., & Patrick, J. (2000). *Education for civic engagement in democracy: Service learning and other promising practices.* Bloomington, IN: ERIC.

Manser, A. (1967). Games and family resemblances. *Philosophy, 42*(161), 210–225.

Marciano, J. (1997). *Civic illiteracy and education: The battle for the hearts and minds of American youth.* New York, NY: Peter Lang.

Mark, M., Henry, G., & Julnes, G. (2000). *Evaluation: An integrated framework for understanding, guiding, and improving policies and programs.* San Francisco, CA: Jossey-Bass.

Marshall, T. H. (1950). *Citizenship and social class, and other essays.* Cambridge, UK: Cambridge University Press.

Mathison, S. (2008). What is the difference between evaluation and research, and why do we care? In N.L. Smith & P.R. Brandon (Eds.) Fundamental issues in evaluation (pp. 183–196). New York, NY: Guilford Press.

Mathison, S. (2000). Promoting democracy through evaluation. In D. Hursch & E.W. Ross (Eds.) *Democratic social education: Social studies for social change.* New York, NY: Falmer Press.

Mattessich, P. W. (2003). *The manager's guide to program evaluation: Planning, contracting, and managing for useful results.* St. Paul, MN: Wilder Foundation.

Matthews, G. (1992). *Dialogues with children.* Cambridge, MA: Harvard University Press.

Mattson, K. (2003). *Engaging youth: Combating the apathy of young Americans toward politics.* New York, NY: Century Foundation Press.

Mayall, B. (1994). *Children's childhoods: Observed and experienced.* London, UK: Falmer Press.

Mayall, B. (1996). *Children, health and the social order.* Buckingham, UK: Open University Press.

Mayall, B. (2002). *Towards a sociology for childhood: Thinking from children's lives.* Buckingham, UK: Open University Press.

Mayeroff, M. (1971). *On caring.* New York, NY: Harper Collins.

McIntosh, H., & Youniss, J. (2010). Toward a political theory of political socialization of youth. In L. Sherrod, J. Torney-Purta, & C. A. Flanagan (Eds.), *Handbook of research on civic engagement in youth* (pp. 23–42). Hoboken, NJ: John Wiley.

McIntyre, A. (2000). *Inner-city kids: Adolescents confront life and violence in an urban community.* New York, NY: New York University Press.

McLellan, J. A., & Youniss, J. (2003). Two systems of youth service: Determinants of voluntary and required youth community service. *Journal of Youth and Adolescence, 32*(1), 47–58.

McNiff, J. (2002). *Action research: Principles and practice.* London, UK: RoutledgeFalmer.

Meier, A. R., Cleary, F. D., & Davis, A. M. (1952). *A curriculum for citizenship: A total school approach to citizenship education.* Detroit, MI: Wayne University Press.

Meschke, L., Peter, C., & Bartholomae, S. (2012). Developmentally appropriate practice to promote healthy adolescent development: Integrating research and practice. *Child and Youth Care Forum, 41*(1), 89–108.

Milbank, D. (2002, May 20–26). Learning about rights and responsibilities: Bush advisers push for a revival of civics classes in schools. *Washington Post National Weekly Edition,* p. 31.

Milner, M. ,Jr. (2004). *Freaks, geeks, and cool kids: American teenagers, schools, and the culture of consumption.* London, UK: Routledge.

Moore, N. (2003). What happened to civics? Today's young people are way too disengaged from the political process, according to a survey by the alliance for representative democracy. *State Legislatures, 29*(10), 32–35.

Morrell, E. (2004). *Becoming critical researchers: Literacy and empowerment for urban youth.* New York, NY: Peter Lang.

Morss, J. (1990). *The biologising of childhood: Developmental psychology and the Darwinian myth.* London, UK: Lawrence Erlbaum.

Moseley, M. (1995). The youth service movement: America's trump card in revitalizing democracy. *National Civic Review, 84*(3), 267–271.

Moss, P., & Petrie, P. (2002). *From children's services to children's spaces: Public policy, children and childhood.* London, UK: RoutledgeFalmer.

Nayak, A. (2003). *Race, place and globalization: Youth cultures in a changing world.* New York, NY: Berg.

Neyfakh, L. (2012, May 20). Are we asking the right questions? *Boston Globe*, p. 1.

Niemi, R., & Junn, J. (1998). *Civic education: What makes students learn.* New Haven, CT: Yale University Press.

Niemi, R., & Junn, J. (2005). *Civic education: What makes students learn.* 2nd ed. New Haven, CT: Yale University Press.

Nie, N., Junn, J., & Stehlik-Barry, K. (1996). *Education and democratic citizenship in America.* Chicago, IL: University of Chicago Press.

O'Donoghue, J., & Kirshner, B. (2008). Engaging urban youth in civic practice: Community-based youth organizations as alternative sites for democratic education. In J. S. Bixby & J. L. Pace (Eds.), *Educating democratic citizens in troubled times: Qualitative studies of current efforts* (pp. 227–251). Albany, NY: State University of New York Press.

Orange, D. (2010). *Thinking for clinicians: Philosophical resources for contemporary psychoanalysis and the humanistic psychotherapies.* New York, NY: Routledge.

Ord, J. (2007). *Youth work process, product and practice: Creating an authentic curriculum in work with young people.* Dorset, UK: Russell House.

Park, P., Brydon-Miller, M., Hall, B., and Jackson, T. (1993). *Voices of participatory research in the United States and Canada.* Westport, CT: Bergin & Garvey.

Parker, W. (1990). Assessing citizenship. *Educational Leadership, 48*(3), 17–22.

Patrick, J. (1996). Principles of democracy for the education of citizens. In J. Patrick & L. Pinhey (Eds.), *Resources on civic education for democracy: International perspectives* (pp. 5–17. Bloomington, IN: ERIC Clearinghouse for International Civic Education.

Patrick, J. (2000). Introduction to education for civic engagement in democracy. In S. Mann & J. Patrick (Eds.), *Education for civic engagement in democracy: Service learning and other promising practices* (pp. 1–8). Bloomington, IN: ERIC Clearinghouse for Social Studies/Social Science Education.

Patrick, J. (1967). *Political socialization of American youth: Implications for secondary school social studies.* Washington D.C.: National Council for the Social Studies.

Patton, M. Q. (1997). *Utilization-focused evaluation: The new century text.* Thousand Oaks, CA: Sage.

Payne, M. (2012). "All gas and no brakes:" Helpful metaphor or harmful stereotype? *Journal of Adolescent Research, 27*(1), 3–17.

Percy-Smith, B. (2010). Councils, consultations, communities: Rethinking spaces for children and youth participation. *Children's Geographies, 8*(2), 107–122.

Percy-Smith, B. (2012). Participation as mediation and social learning: Empowering children as actors in social contexts. In C. Baraldi & V. Iervese (Eds.), *Participation, facilitation, and mediation: Children and young people in their social contexts* (pp. .12–29). New York, NY: Routledge.

Percy-Smith, B., & Thomas, N. (2010). *A handbook of children and young people's participation: Perspectives from theory and practice.* New York, NY: Routledge.

Polanyi, M. (1958). *Personal knowledge: Toward a post-critical philosophy.* New York, NY: Routledge.

Polkinghorne, D. (1988). *Narrative knowing and the human sciences.* Albany, NY: State University of New York Press.

Pratte, R. (1988). *The civic imperative: Examining the need for civic education.* New York, NY: Teachers College Press.

Pufall, P., & Unsworth, R. (2004). *Rethinking childhood.* New Brunswick, NJ: Rutgers University Press.

Purdy, L. (1992). *In their best interest? The case against equal rights for children.* Ithaca, NY: Cornell University Press.

Putnam, R. (1995). Bowling alone: America's declining social capital. *Journal of Democracy, 6*(1), 65–78.

Putnam, R. (2000). *Bowling alone.* New York, NY: Simon & Schuster.

Rafferty, S. (2001). *Giving children a voice—what next? A study from one primary school.* Retrieved from The Scottish Council for Research in Education Web site, http://www.scre.ac.uk

Ravitch, D. (1997). Better than alternatives. *Society, 34*(2), 29–31.

Ravitch, D. (2002). Diversity, tragedy, and the schools. *Brookings Review, 20*(1), 2–4.

Reason, P. (Ed). (1994). *Participation in human inquiry.* Thousand Oaks, CA: Sage.

Reiman, A., Sprinthall, N., & Thies-Sprinthall, L. (1999). The conceptual and ethical development of teachers. In R. Mosher, D. Youngman, & J. Day (Eds.), *Human development across the life span* (pp. 203–218). Westport, CT: Praeger.

Rizvi, Z. (2012). *In search of safety and solutions: Somali refugee adolescent girls at Sheder and Aw Barre camps, Ethiopia.* New York, NY: Women's Refugee Commission.

Rogers, J., Mediratta, K., & Shah, S. (2012). Building power, learning democracy: Youth organizing as a site of civic development. *Review of Research in Education, 36*(1), 43–66.

Rogers, P., & Williams, B. (2006). Evaluation for practice improvement and organizational learning. In I. Shaw, J. Greene, & M. Mark (Eds.), *The Sage handbook of evaluation* (pp. 76–97). London, UK: Sage.

Rogoff, B. (1990). *Apprenticeship in thinking: Cognitive development in social context.* New York, NY: Oxford University Press.

Rogoff, B. (2003). *The cultural nature of human development.* Oxford, UK: Oxford University Press.

Rossi, P. H., Freeman, H. E., & Lipsey, M. W. (2003). *Evaluation: A systematic approach.* London: Sage.

Rubin, B. (2007). There's still not justice: Youth civic identity development amid distinct school and community contexts. *Teachers College Record, 109*(2), 449–481.

Russel, W.F. (1950). The citizenship education project. *Teachers College Record, 52*(2), 77–89.

Ryan, K. E., & DeStefano, L. (2000). *Evaluation as a democratic process: Promoting inclusion, dialogue, and deliberation.* San Francisco, CA: Jossey-Bass.

Sabo, K. (2003). *Youth participatory evaluation: A field in the making.* San Francisco, CA: Jossey-Bass.

Sabo Flores, K. (2008). *Youth participatory evaluation: Strategies for engaging young people.* San Francisco, CA: Jossey-Bass.

Schon, D. (1983). *The reflective practitioner: How professionals think in action.* New York, NY: Basic Books.

Schutz, A., & Sandy, M. (2011). *Collective action for social change: An introduction to community organizing.* Hampshire, UK: Palgrave Macmillan.

Scott, M., & Lyman, S. (1968). Accounts. *American Sociological Review, 33*(1), 46–62.

Sehr, D. (1997). *Education for public democracy.* Albany, NY: State University of New York Press.

Sherrod, L., Flanagan, C., & Youniss, J. (2002). Dimensions of citizenship and opportunities for youth development: The what, why, when, where, and who of citizenship development. *Applied Developmental Science, 6*(4), 264–272.

Shumer, R. (2013). Engaging youth in the evaluation process. In R. VeLure Roholt, M. Baizerman, & R.W. Hildreth (Eds.) *Civic youth work: Cocreating democratic youth spaces* (pp. 55–66). Chicago, IL: Lyceum Press.

Shumer, R. (2007). *Youth-led evaluation: A guidebook.* Clemson, SC: National Dropout Prevention Center.

Simon, J. & Merrill, B. (1998). Political socialization in the classroom revisited: The kids voting program. *The Social Science Journal, 35*(1), 29–42.

Singh, A., & Salazar, C. (2011). *Social justice in group work: Practical interventions for change.* New York, NY: Routledge.

Skelton, T. (2008). Children, young people, UNICEF and participation. In S. Aitken, R. Lund, & A. T. Kjorholt (Eds.), *Global childhoods: Globalization, development and young people* (pp. 165–182). New York, NY: Routledge.

Skelton, T., & Valentine, G. (1998). *Cool places: Geographies of youth cultures.* London, UK: Routledge.

Skelton, N., Boyte, H., & Sordelet Leonard, L. (2002). *Youth civic engagement: Reflections on an emerging public idea.* Minneapolis, MN: Center for Democracy and Citizenship.

Skott-Myhre, H. (2006). Radical youth work: Becoming visible. *Child and Youth Care Forum, 35*(3), 219–229.

Sloam, J. (2012). New voice, less equal: The civic and political engagement of young people in the United States and Europe. *Comparative Political Studies*, 1–26. Advance online publication. doi: 10.1177/0010414012453441

Smith, M. (1982). *Creators not consumers: Rediscovering social education.* Leicester, UK: National Association of Youth Clubs.

Smith, M., & Jeffs, T. (1999). *Informal education: Conversation, democracy and learning.* Derbyshire, UK: Education Now.

Spelman, E. (2003). *Repair.* Boston, MA: Beacon Press.

Stainton Rogers, R. (2004). Constructing a way of life. In J. Roche, S. Tucker, R. Thomson, & R. Flynn (Eds.), *Youth in society* (pp. 177–183). London, UK: Sage.

Stainton Rogers, W. (2001). Theories of child development. In P. Foley, J. Roche, & S. Tucker (Eds.), *Children in society: Contemporary theory, policy and practice* (pp. 202–214). New York, NY: Palgrave Macmillan.

Stoper, E. (1977). The Student Nonviolent Coordinating Committee: The rise and fall of a redemptive organization. *Journal of Black Studies, 8*(1), 13–34.

Storrie, T. (2004). Citizens or what? In J. Roche, S. Tucker, R. Thomson, & R. Flynn (Eds.), *Youth in society* (pp. 52–60). London, UK: Sage.

Strama, M. (1998). Overcoming cynicism: Youth participation and electoral politics. *National Civic Review, 87*(1), 71–78.

Stringer, E. (1996). *Action research: A handbook for practitioners.* Thousand Oaks, CA: Sage.

Stuart, C. (2012). *Foundations of child and youth care.* Dubuque, IA: Kendall Hunt.

Suárez-Orozco, M., & Qin-Hilliard, D. (2004). *Globalization culture and education in the new millennium.* Berkeley, CA: University of California Press.

Tait, G. (2000). *Youth, sex and government.* New York, NY: Peter Lang.

Teenage girl wins a seat in Uganda's parliament. (2012, September 18). *The Guardian.* Retrieved from http://www.guardian.co.uk/world/feedarticle/10443948

Terry, A. W., & Bohnenberger, J. E. (2003). Service learning: Fostering a cycle of caring in our gifted youth. *Journal of Secondary Gifted Education, 15*(1), 23–32.

Thau, R., & Eisinger, R. M. (2000, April 26). Younger voters get short shrift. *USA Today,* p. 17a.

Thompson, K. (1998). *Moral panics.* London, UK: Routledge.

Thurston, H.W. (1947). *The education of youth as citizens.* New York, NY: R.R. Smith.

Tillberg, P. (2006). Some aspects of military practices and officers' professional skill. In B. Göranzon, M. Hammaren, & R. Ennals (Eds.), *Dialogue, skill, and tacit knowledge* (pp. 152–174). Chichester, UK: J. Wiley.

Underwood, G. (Ed.). (1996). *Implicit cognition.* Oxford, UK: Oxford University Press.

Utter, G. (2011). *Youth and political participation: A reference handbook.* Santa Barbara, CA: ABC-CLIO.

van Manen, M. (1990). *Researching lived experience: Human science for an action sensitive pedagogy.* Albany, NY: State University of New York Press.

VeLure Roholt, R., Baizerman, M., & Hildreth, R.W. (2013). *Civic youth work: Co-creating democratic youth spaces*. Chicago, IL: Lyceum Press.

VeLure Roholt, R., Hildreth, R. W., & Baizerman, M. (2008). The place of evaluation. *Child and Youth Services, 29*(3–4), 71–82.

VeLure Roholt, R., McFall, L., Baizerman, M., & Smith, P. (2009). *Building democracy with young people in contested spaces: A handbook for critically reflective practice that challenges cultures of violence*. Belfast, Northern Ireland: Public Achievement Northern Ireland.

VeLure Roholt, R., Hildreth, R.W., & Baizerman, M. (2009). *Becoming citizens: Deepening the craft of youth civic engagement*. New York, NY: Routledge Press.

Verma, R. (2010). *Be the change: Teacher, activist, global citizen*. New York, NY: Peter Lang.

Waterman, A. (Ed.). (1997). *Service-learning: Applications from the research*. Mahwah, NJ: Lawrence Erlbaum.

Way, N. (1998). *Everyday courage: The lives and stories of urban teenagers*. New York, NY: New York University Press.

Weiss, C. (1998). *Evaluation* (2nd Edition). Upper Saddle River, NJ: Prentice Hall.

Weller, S. (2007). *Teenagers' citizenship: Experiences and education*. New York, NY: Routledge.

Wells, G. (1999). *Dialogic inquiry: Towards a sociocultural practice and theory of education*. Cambridge, UK: Cambridge University Press.

Wenger, E. (1998). *Communities of practice: Learning, meaning, and identity*. Cambridge,UK: Cambridge University Press.

Wichowsky, A. (2002).The importance of civic education. Retrieved from http://www.cived.net/tioce.html.

Winter, N. (2003). Social capital, civic engagement and positive youth development outcomes. Retrieved from http://www.policystudies.com/studies/community/Civic%-20Engagement.pdf

Wolcott, H. (1999). *Ethnography: A way of seeing*. Lanham, MD: Altamira Press.

Worthen, B., Sanders, J. R., & Fitzpatrick, J. L. (1997). *Program evaluation: Alternative approaches and practical guidelines* (2nd ed.). New York, NY: Longman.

Wren,B. (1977). *Education for justice: Pedagogical principles*. Maryknoll, NY: Orbis Books.

Wyatt Knowlton, L., & Phillips, C. (2013). *The logic model guidebook: Better strategies for great results*. Thousand Oaks, CA: Sage.

Wyn, J., & White, R. (1997). *Rethinking youth*. Thousand Oaks, CA: Sage.

Wyness, M. (2000). *Contesting childhood*. London, UK: Falmer Press.

Yates, M., & Youniss, J. (Eds.). (1999). *Roots of civic identity: International perspectives on community service and activism in youth*. Cambridge, UK: Cambridge University Press.

Young, S., Richards-Schuster, K., Davis, A., & Pellegrine, I. (2013). Creating spaces for the next generation of civil rights in Mississippi: Youth participation in the Mississippi safe schools coalition. In R. VeLure Roholt, M. Baizerman, & R.W. Hildreth (Eds.). *Civic youth work: Co-creating democratic youth spaces* (pp. 43–54). Chicago, IL: Lyceum Press.

Youniss, J., McLellan, J., & Yates, M. (1997). What we know about engendering civic identity. *American Behavioral Scientist, 40*(5), 620–632.

Youniss, J., & Yates, M. (1997). Community service and social responsibility in youth. Chicago, IL: University of Chicago Press.

Zaff, J., Malanchuk, E., Michelsen, E., & Eccles, J. (2003, March). *Socializing youth for citizenship.* Circle Working Paper 03. College Park, MD: CIRCLE.

Zeiser, P. (2001). Building better citizens: Increasing the level of civic education among teens in Jacksonville, Florida. *National Civic Review, 90*(3), 289–291.

Zeldin, S., Camino, L., & Calvert, M. (2003). Toward an understanding of youth in community governance: Policy priorities and research directions. *Social Policy Report, 17*(3), 3–20.

Zeldin, S., McDaniel, A., Topitzes, D., & Calvert, M. (2000). *Youth in decision-making: A study on the impacts of youth on adults and organizations.* Madison, WI: Innovation Center.

Zukin, C., Keeter, S., Andolina, M., Jenkins, K., & Delli Carpini, M. (2006). *A new engagement?: Political participation, civic life, and the changing American citizen.* New York, NY: Oxford University Press.

Index

A

Action, 2, 10–14, 17, 24–30, 38, 46, 73,
    101–103, 118
    Civic, 14, 52–55, 57–59, 62–64, 105
    Citizen, 85
    Collective, 80, 94
    Community, 54, 59
    Competence, 29
    Group, 13, 37, 66, 76, 83–84, 103, 105
    Learning, 11, 63
    Political, 34, 65
    Research, 44, 65
    Social, 10, 14, 54, 55, 82–83,
    Youth, 11
Activated, 94–96
Activism, 7, 15, 17–18, 67, 103,
    Youth, 11, 16–17, 52, 56,
Activist, 14, 66,
    Civic, 102
    Young people as, 12, 26–27,
Addressed, 78, 88, 93, 101–102,

Adolescence, 9, 21–23, 47, 66, 75
Adults as Allies, 59
Advice-giving, 10, 56, 188
Advocacy, 44,
Age, 15, 21–26
Ageism, 15, 70
Agency, 22, 25, 47, 82
Agents, 24, 45, 55, 70
Aitken, Stuart 19–20, 24, 26–27
Animate, 69,
    Animating, 108, 129
Ansell, Nicola, 24, 123
Apathetic, 30–31, 87, 100
Appadurai, Arjun, 62, 65, 123
Argyris, Chris, 63, 123
Atomists, 104

B

Banking Education, 63
Battistoni, Richard, 11, 42, 124, 125
Becoming, 77, 88

Citizen, 16, 85, 95–96, 98–99
Being, 19, 26, 89, 94
 In-The-World, 24, 25,
 Citizen, 27–28, 67, 83, 85, 88, 99
 Civic youth worker, 104–105
Benner, Patricia, 94, 124
Bensman, Joseph, 12, 104, 124
Bidirectionality, 22,
Biophysiological, 20–22, 50, 75,
Boal, Agusto, 54, 125
Boyte, Harry, 7, 11, 32–34, 39, 43–44, 60,
 99, 102–103, 125, 128, 136
Buber, Martin, 89, 100, 119, 121, 125

C

Called, 78, 94
 To an issue, 102,
 To citizenship, 8,
Capability Approach, 50, 68, 94, 107
Celebrating, 74, 86
Change the World, 17, 44–45, 52–55,
 57–60, 62–64, 74–89, 102,
 Levels of Change, 96, 112–117
 Personal Change, 102
Chawla, Louise, 38, 44, 126
Checkoway, Barry, 11, 21, 24, 31–32, 44–45,
 59, 94, 114, 117–119, 126, 128
Chilcoat, George, 29, 44–45, 53–55, 126
Childhood, 24, 26,
Chilisa, Bagele, 62, 126
Citizen, 8, 10, 28–29, 30–32, 79,
 Citizen Work, 7–8, 102
 Citizen-Making Gaze, 9–10, 95–96
 Democratic, 30, 76, 84, 103
 Development, 9–10, 75, 83–90, 94, 95,
  98–99, 101–104, 114, 117
 Young People As, 2, 11–12, 15–17,
  19–21, 26–27, 29–32, 73, 98
 Youth, 32–33, 66–69, 70, 79, 82
Citizenship, 14–16, 19
 Democratic, 28–32, 84, 88, 114
 Education, 11, 14, 38–49, 56,
 Lifelong, 11

Lived, 7–9, 12, 17, 79, 82–85,
Public work, 33–34
Youth, 20–21, 37–38, 52, 56, 60–61,
 64–65
Civic Education, 40–41
Civility, 123
Coach(ing), 11, 85, 106
Cocreate, 6, 25, 29, 66, 73, 100–102, 106
Coevaluators, 118
Collaborative, 2, 64–65, 70, 90,
Collective Work, 33, 82, 90
Communitarian, 28
Communitas, 75, 90
Community Service, 42
Concern, 74
Conductor, 105
Constructivist, 20–21, 23–24, 26–27, 44
Consultant, 106
Coresearchers, 64
Craft Orientation, 2, 8, 9, 12, 17, 66, 74, 79,
 83, 93–95, 120
Critical Education, 56–57

D

Darwinian, 133
de Tocqueville, Alexis, 14, 82, 127
Delgado, Melvin, 44, 66, 127
Deliberation
 In Evaluation, 118–120
Democratic
 Space, 2, 59, 74–77, 106, 108, 120
 Work, 16, 34, 55, 57, 62, 84–86,
Denaturalization, 124
Dewey, John, 29, 33, 41, 127
Deweyian, 33
Dialogic, 18, 123, 138
Dialogue, 45, 100, 118–121, 125, 128–129,
 137
Disenfranchisement, 55, 68, 70
Disengagement, 10, 100, 133
Dreyfus, Stuart, 95–96, 127

E

Educative, 129
Emancipatory, 64, 126
Embody, 34, 67, 69, 103, 84, 124
Empower, 44,53, 63, 134,
Ethics, 7, 13, 63, 74, 94, 107, 120, 124, 127, 135
Ethos, 9–10, 16, 44, 66–67, 74, 83–84, 93–94, 99–100, 104, 119–120
Evaluative, 85
Everyday Life, 13,49, 67, 95
Evolving Capacities, 131
Existential, 22, 78, 80, 99
Experiential Learning, 63
Expertise, 4, 13, 85, 95–97, 104–106, 115, 127–128, 130

F

Facilitator, 105
Farr, James, 7, 11, 32–33, 43, 60, 99, 103, 125
Fine, Michelle, 11, 44–45, 64–65, 125
Freedom Schools, 44–45, 52–57
Freire, Paulo, 13, 40, 53, 59, 72, 99, 117, 124–126
Friedman, Maurice, 15, 90, 95–96, 124

G

Gadamer, Hans, 48, 128
Gaze, 9, 17, 74, 95
Ginwright, Shawn, 11, 45, 55–56, 128–127, 131
Giroux, Henry, 107, 129
Globalisation, 123, 134, 136–137
Grassroots, 55
Group Work, 13, 58, 76, 82–85,
Guide, 54, 105

H

Hart, Roger, 32, 34–37, 44, 61, 103, 119, 129
Healthy Youth Development, 16, 45–48, 66,
Hermeneutic, 34, 107, 126
Homogenizing, 48
Horton, Miles, 76, 130
Human Development, 49, 75, 84, 135

I

Identity, 102
    Civic, 37, 45–46,
    Group, 102,
Inclusive, 9, 18, 56, 60, 80, 85, 94, 96, 100, 101, 103, 106
Indigenous, 62, 126
Informal Education, 59
Intentional Practice, 12, 77, 79, 94, 98,
Intergenerational, 37, 56
Involvement
    Active, 10
    Citizen, 9, 19
    Youth, 10–11, 15–16, 34–37, 52, 59–60,

J

Jeffs, Tony, 23, 24–24, 32, 41, 130, 137

K

Kolb, David, 98, 103, 131
Konopka, Gisela, 82, 84–85, 131
Ladder Of Participation, 34–37, 61
Lansdown, Gerison, 22, 32, 35, 59, 94, 131
Leadership 82, 100
    Civic, 64,
    Group, 113
    Youth 2, 46,
Lesko, Nancy, 20–25, 132

Lighthouse, 106
Lilienfeld, Robert, 12, 104, 124
Lived Experience, 17, 50, 53, 54, 57, 137

M

Males, Mike, 55, 100, 132
Marginalize, 16, 68–69
Mastery, 96–98

N

Noguera, Pedro, 11, 45, 55–56, 129, 131
Nonengagement, 10–11
Nonparticipation, 14–15, 34–36, 38, 40, 61,
Nonviolent, 56, 83, 94, 100, 101, 103, 141
Novice, 96

O

Outcome, 8, 112–120, 121
Outputs, 116

P

Participatory Action Research, 62, 65,
Patton, Michael, Q., 112, 125, 134
Phenomenological, 79, 90, 104
Phronesis, 90, 93–94, 96, 99, 107
Plasticity, 22
Positivism, 48, 90
Power, 12, 17, 47, 82, 121
    Between Adults and Young People,
        37–38, 70, 117
Praxis, 7, 17, 69, 89, 93, 95
Public, 79,
    Issues, 2, 10, 65, 86, 100–101
    Work, 7, 8, 11, 33–34, 37–38, 44, 60, 88,
        98–99
PUKAR, 52, 62–65

R

Reason, Peter, 2, 64–65, 135
Recapitulation, 22, 50
Reflection, 17, 81–82, 86, 101,
    In Action Research, 65
    In Service Learning, 43,
Rehearsal Space, 9, 75, 85, 91
Repair, 10, 86, 137

S

Service learning, 11, 41–43
SNCC, 56–57
Social capital, 14, 56, 70, 99, 113, 117

T

Tacit Knowledge, 5–6, 18, , 22
Techne, 89, 99
Telos, 23, 49
Theater Of The Oppressed, 54, 129
Tokenism, 36, 61, 129
Touchstone, 9, 66, 85, 89, 93, 99–104, 108,
    116, 128

U

United Nations Convention on the Rights
    of The Child, 25, 59, 70
Utilization, 114, 120, 121, 134

V

Van Manen, Max, 24, 48, 103–104, 137
Vocation, 17, 102
Volunteering, 40–43

W

Wisdom, 3, 8, 49, 91, 94, 98, 100, 111

Political, 87
Practical, 90, 94,
Practice, 45, 96, 107

Y

Youth Image, 1213, 19–24, 27, 48, 50
Youth Rights, 32, 34–35, 59–61, 67, 70, 102,
   104, 118
Youth Voice, 19, 34–35, 37–38, 67, 70
Youth Vote, 28, 31
Youthhood, 24, 26–27, 50
Youth-led, 16
   Evaluation, 64, 117–120
   Grant-making, 57
Youth Participatory (Action) Research, 11,
   64–65, 71
Youth Work,
   As Ballet, 94, 105
   As Jazz, 44, 94, 104

Peter Lang PRIMERS
in Education

Peter Lang Primers are designed to provide a brief and concise introduction or supplement to specific topics in education. Although sophisticated in content, these primers are written in an accessible style, making them perfect for undergraduate and graduate classroom use. Each volume includes a glossary of key terms and a References and Resources section.

Other published and forthcoming volumes cover such topics as:

- Standards
- Popular Culture
- Critical Pedagogy
- Literacy
- Higher Education
- John Dewey
- Feminist Theory and Education

- Studying Urban Youth Culture
- Multiculturalism through Postformalism
- Creative Problem Solving
- Teaching the Holocaust
- Piaget and Education
- Deleuze and Education
- Foucault and Education

Look for more Peter Lang Primers to be published soon. To order other volumes, please contact our Customer Service Department:

       800-770-LANG (within the US)
       212-647-7706 (outside the US)
       212-647-7707 (fax)

To find out more about this and other Peter Lang book series, or to browse a full list of education titles, please visit our website:
       www.peterlang.com